Birds of the Heart

Birds of the Heart

by

Galya Gunderson

GR

George Ronald
Oxford

George Ronald, *Publisher*
46 High Street, Kidlington, Oxford OX5 2DN

A catalogue record for this book is available from the British Library

ISBN 0-85398-432-8

Typeset by Sonehaven Press, Knoxville, Tennessee
Cover designed by Alexander Leith
Printed in Great Britain by Redwood Books

Contents

Acknowledgements

My sincere thanks and appreciation to

the Bahá'ís of La Selva Beach, California for their on-going encouragement

my Oregon friends

Peggy Monschke
Cathy McDonald
Susan Brand
Poppy McCuistion

for their continuing enthusiasm and

the staff and library at the Bosch Bahá'í School, located in the Santa Cruz Mountains of Northern California, for training and resources.

To the loving memory of

Bahiyyeh Khan

beloved daughter of
Ali Kuli Khan

Preface

> From the continual imitation of ancient and worn-out ways, the world had grown dark as darksome night. The fundamentals of the divine Teaching had passed from memory; their pith and heart had been totally forgotten, and the people were holding on to husks. The nations had, like tattered garments long outworn, fallen into a pitiful condition.
>
> Out of this pitch blackness there dawned the morning splendour of the Teachings of Bahá'u'lláh. He hath dressed the world with a garment new and fair, and that new garment is the principles which have come down from God.
>
> *'Abdu'l-Bahá*[1]

During the Native American Pioneering Conference at the San Francisco Bahá'í Center, January 1992, a simple request was made: 'Name some of the basic principles of the Bahá'í Faith.' I discovered, much to my embarrassment, that I could only come up with two or three of these on the spur of the moment.

After much reflection, later at home, I made a decision to master these principles, to learn them by heart, and to memorize an elucidating passage from the writings of Bahá'u'lláh for each principle.

The days of the fast that year were happily spent in 'mining' passages from various sources and sharing these with the Bahá'ís of La Selva Beach. We came to the conclusion at that time that a book of this nature might be of great help to Bahá'í youth and a travelling companion for young pioneers.

First I used the list of principles 'Abdu'l-Bahá had brought to the attention of the West at the beginning of the 20th century. Later it was suggested that I add those spiritual principles to which the Universal House of Justice had recently given emphasis.

To assist the reader in the process of memorization, contemplation, teaching and sharing with others, I have included 'Keys for Unlocking the Creative Word', a guide adapted from the Ruhi Institute programme and expanded to aid memorization and use of the quotations.

The title *Birds of the Heart* is meant to evoke the radiant flight of the creative Word into the receptive hearts of humankind. It is my sincere hope that you will find this book of help to you on your journey into the sacred writings of our beloved Faith.

Galya Gunderson
Hidden Caves Retreat
Cascadia, Oregon
February 1999

Introduction

One winter evening Bahiyyeh (Hamideh) Khan and I drove through the woods together enjoying the trees and the crisp mountain air. We arrived at the small town of Boulder Cross in the Santa Cruz mountains and decided to explore a bit as the lights in the shop windows were warm and inviting.

We found the 'All and Everything' store especially intriguing and Bahiyyeh, after trying on a hat or two, discovered the book section. The proprietor came, at this time, to assist her and she asked if he had any Bahá'í books in stock. He replied that he was sorry that he didn't but expressed some knowledge of and interest in the Bahá'í Faith.

Suddenly my little friend began to change. No longer was she the old and infirm woman I knew. She seemed to be illumined and in motion . . . a radiant being, incandescent and superbly alive. Words poured forth from her like iridescent birds soaring above some enchanted garden . . . and the small shop appeared to bloom with a wondrous light and life. Those of us who were in her presence have never forgotten that night.

Birds of the Heart was inspired by Bahiyyeh Khan, who taught me how very important it is to know the words of Bahá'u'lláh by heart.

1

Keys for Unlocking the Creative Word

> The Word of God is the king of words and its pervasive influence is incalculable. It hath ever dominated and will continue to dominate the realm of being. The Great Being saith: The Word is the master key for the whole world, inasmuch as through its potency the doors of the hearts of men, which in reality are the doors of heaven, are unlocked . . . It is an ocean inexhaustible in riches, comprehending all things.
>
> *Bahá'u'lláh*[1]

The key to unlocking the human heart is the Word of God. Yet some of us have difficulty understanding the words of the sacred writings, in recalling them exactly and applying them in our lives.

Our appreciation, recollection, use and application of the sacred writings can be greatly enhanced if we can find a way to make them more accessible to us. The following is but one suggested approach.

Keys that Unlock the Writings

Understanding

1. Read the selection.

2. Meditate upon the inner meaning.
3. Write out the selection.
4. Underline the key words.
5. Formulate and write a question for each phrase or idea.
6. Answer your question with a direct quotation from the text.

Memorization

7. Create and write your own symbolic code for the selection.
8. Recall the selection using your code.
9. Refer to the text to check for accuracy.
10. Recite your selection every day using code or text as necessary.

Utilization

11. Find as many ways as you can to incorporate the creative Word into your daily conversation at gatherings, firesides, teaching events, lectures, etc.
12. Deepen continually on the creative Word. Through meditation and contemplation strive to make these words a living and creative part of yourself.

Understanding

> O young trees and plants, matchless and tender, that grow in the meadows of guidance! O ye newcomers to the Fraternity of Truth!
>
> Although now ye be learners, the hope is that through showerings from the clouds of grace, ye will become teachers; that ye will flourish even as flowers and fragrant herbs in the garden of that knowledge which is both of the mind and of the heart; that each one of you will grow as a tree rich in yield, fair, fresh and strong, heavy with sweet fruit. *'Abdu'l-Bahá*[2]

> Enter, O people, beneath the shelter of the Word! Then drink therefrom the choice wine of inner significances and utterances; for therein is hidden the kawthar of the glorious One – and it hath appeared from the horizon of the Will of your Lord, the merciful, with wonderful lights. *Bahá'u'lláh*[3]

> > kawthar (co-sair) abundance. Traditionally, a lake or river in paradise which Anas relates Muḥammad saw on the night on His Mir'áj as 'a river of water on each side of which there were domes, each formed of a hollow pearl'.
> > *Marzieh Gail*[4]

As you begin working with the creative Word, from time to time you will come across a word, such as kawthar, which you will be unable to locate in your dictionary, and yet the meaning of this word may well be essential to the understanding of the selection you are studying.

If you do not have a reference work that defines these words in your Bahá'í library, you can consult your Bahá'í librarian or call your Publishing Trust and they will help you in the selection of a good reference volume for this purpose which is currently available.

Think how impoverished our understanding of this beautiful verse would have been had we not learned that the kawthar is the hidden river of paradise, surrounded by domes of hollow pearls, hollow to be filled with understanding – understanding of and appreciation for the abundance and inner significance of the Word of God and His holy utterance.

Step 1: Read the selection

Choose a verse from the writings that deeply appeals to you and read it. You will probably come across some words which are new or foreign to you or whose meaning you are not sure of. At this point your best friend and companion will be your dictionary. It should be a comprehensive one, the best you can find. If the print in the dictionary is small and hard to read, consider investing in a good rectangular magnifying glass.

It may be a good plan to make a list of these words as you come across them and even jot down the appropriate definitions from your dictionary. This will help you remember the correct meanings when you come across them again, as you most likely will.

You may think this takes a lot of time and effort but a little work at this stage will pay great dividends. It is much easier to establish correct understanding in the beginning than to root out inaccurate shades of meaning later on.

Now read your verse again and note the difference in your understanding.

You should feel comfortable with *all* the words now and experience a certain joy of accomplishment.

Step 2: Meditate upon the inner meaning

Meditate. What does *that* mean? First of all, switching to a special level of mind is required.

Scientists have identified four basic human states of mind and labelled them Beta, Alpha, Theta and Delta. They know these states exist because the brain wave patterns generated at each of these levels are quite different and measurable on the sensitive machines used in research.

In step 1 we were actively using our Beta state of ordinary waking consciousness. This is the state we use when dealing with the outer world: gathering information, solving problems and communicating in general. This state is also prone to the many distractions and disruptions existing around us, together with our own sometimes erratic thought patterns. It is impossible to *experience* the creative Word at this level of consciousness. It would be like trying to listen to an exquisitely beautiful and profound piece of music on a radio station which frequently interposed news reports, static, weather updates and advertising into its programmes. You could recognize that music was being played – you might even determine the selection and the composer – but there is no way that you could experience the incredible beauty and depth of the music that the composer created. Your response would likely be frustration and confusion, perhaps a decision that you did not like the music anyway, prompting you to switch off the radio or change stations.

You may wonder why it is so difficult for us to achieve the beautiful depth of communion Bahá'u'lláh alludes to in the following passage:

> Meditate on what the poet hath written: 'Wonder not, if my Best-Beloved be closer to me than mine own self; wonder at this, that I, despite such nearness, should still be so far from Him.'[5]

Perhaps this is because meditation requires the deeper Alpha and Theta states of mind. You have experienced these deeper states before. Remember that great movie on television? You were comfortable, at home, so relaxed. Gradually you began to experience that movie; you were *there*, fully enjoying being a part of everything that was happening on the screen. You were totally detached from and unaware of your environment. Your whole focus was the state of 'being in the film' and your concentration was single-pointed.

This is the state of mind that we use when we experience the creative Word. Using the creative Word as a platform of focus and the Alpha → Theta state as a springboard, we will be able to dive into 'an ocean in whose depths are concealed innumerable pearls of great price, of surpassing lustre'.[6]

Remember that single-pointed concentration is the key. As 'Abdu'l-Bahá tells us, 'So long as the thoughts of an individual are scattered he will achieve no results, but if his thinking be concentrated on a single point wonderful will be the fruits thereof.'[7]

This journey will not be easy. It requires energy, determination, perseverance and detachment so that we can attain and remain in this state of single-pointed concentration and reflection at will.

Hit the surface and you will be immersed in the distractions of Beta; dive too deeply and you will find yourself in the drowsy pre-sleep stages of low Theta or the deep 'out there' sleep of Delta, where all the 'pearls' are forgotten.

In the beginning you will probably have just a taste now and then of what it will be like later when you have mastered the state and concentration required for deep communion. Please do not be discouraged! Persevere in your efforts, keep in training, for the Blessed Beauty Himself has promised you these 'pearls of great price'. Continue your diving and you shall soon have them.

Step 3: Write out the selection

While writing out your selection, try to stay centred on the creative Word. The act of writing will then reinforce your knowledge and understanding.

You should maintain an attitude of profound respect and belief in the Word of God during this exercise for, as the Báb so graciously promises us:

> Every hand which setteth down His Words with true faith shall be filled by God, both in this world and in the next, with things that are highly prized . . .[8]

You may wish to consider starting a special book containing your own favourite selections from the writings set in your own handwriting.

Step 4: Underline the key words

Key words are the building blocks of meaning in your verse. Without the key words, the verse would consist of only connective and descriptive words and would be utterly meaningless.

Suppose you have chosen to work with a phrase from the writings of 'Abdu'l-Bahá: 'Truthfulness is the foundation of all human virtues.'[9]

This phrase is full of key words. You will need to underline 'truthfulness', 'foundation', 'human' and 'virtues'. Each of the words you have underlined has a meaning which is critical to unlocking the message of the whole verse. Leave out just one of these key words and the meaning will be changed.

Step 5. Formulate and write a question for each phrase or idea

Working with the whole quotation this time, think of a question for each idea it contains and write it down. For example, use the same verse from 'Abdu'l-Bahá:

> Truthfulness is the foundation of all human virtues. Without truthfulness, progress and success, in all the worlds of God, are impossible for any soul. When this holy attribute is established in man, all the divine qualities will also be acquired.[10]

Now for the questions:

a. What is truthfulness?

b. What would happen to the progress of a soul without truthfulness?

c. What will happen when truthfulness is established in man?

Step 6. Answer your question with a direct quotation from the text.

Now you are ready to answer the three questions, using the text itself:

> Question: What is truthfulness?
> Answer from the text: 'Truthfulness is the foundation of all human virtues.'
>
> Question: What would happen to the progress of a soul without truthfulness?
> Answer from the text: 'Without truthfulness, progress and success, in all the worlds of God, are impossible for any soul.'
>
> Question: What will happen when truthfulness is established in man?
> Answer from the text: 'When this holy attribute is established in man, all the divine qualities will also be acquired.'

You are now finished with the first section. This would perhaps be a good time to take a moment to think about what you have learned so far and see what you might wish to do with this knowledge. You might want to ask yourself some questions about the theme of this section, practising honesty in your answers.

Your questions might run something like this:

- How important do I think it is to acquire this attribute?
- Do I really want to acquire this attribute?
- What changes will that require in my attitudes and behaviour?
- Am I really willing to make these changes?
- When do I plan to begin?
- What do I expect to happen if I am successful?

This is an example of the type of reflection that will enable you to use the creative Word as a guideline and catalyst for change in your own spiritual growth and development.

Now you have finished the first six steps of your programme, ask yourself, 'Do I understand my chosen verse better?' If so, you are ready to begin to memorize it.

Memorization

> The sanctified souls should ponder and meditate in their hearts regarding the methods of teaching. From the texts of the wondrous, heavenly Scriptures they should memorize phrases and passages bearing on various instances, so that in the course of their speech they may recite divine verses whenever the occasion demandeth it, inasmuch as these holy verses are the most potent elixir, the greatest and mightiest talis-

> man. So potent is their influence that the hearer will have no cause for vacillation. I swear by My life! This Revelation is endowed with such a power that it will act as the lodestone for all nations and kindreds of the earth.[11]

In this quotation Bahá'u'lláh emphasizes the importance for our teaching work of memorizing phrases and passages from the writings. How often have I wished for just the right phrase to illustrate a principle of the Faith when the moment presented itself and how often have I found myself lacking these precious words.

Some of us have great difficulty memorizing verses. We want to follow the directive of Bahá'u'lláh and become excellent Bahá'í teachers but we are filled with feelings of inadequacy and self doubt. Where do we begin? It is all so complicated! 'I don't have enough time!' we cry. But it is simple, really. All we need to do is memorize an appropriate phrase and we have begun! As we immerse ourselves in the creative Word, our confidence grows along with natural opportunities for expression. Even if you have just five or ten minutes a day, the key is consistency. A great deal can be accomplished in a short time if you set your goals and persevere each day.

Since the root of memory lies in the subconscious mind and the language of the subconscious mind is symbols, why not use symbols to increase retentive memory? This is exactly what we will do in the next step.

When you have understood and mastered the steps in this section you may wish to share them with others. Perhaps your grandmother cannot remember her favourite prayer: What joy it would bring to her heart if you could help her to do this by sharing your knowledge and techniques.

Step 7: Create and write your own symbolic code for the selection

In this step we create a symbolic code by taking a key word in a phrase and drawing a symbol above the word that represents the meaning of that word to your mind. It is important that your symbol has meaning for you and is not the idea of someone else.

Continue to work through the quotation, using as many symbols for key words as you wish, thereby creating your own visually symbolic code. You may find later that recalling just one key symbol such as ♥ may help you to remember a whole phrase or an even longer passage.

Those who have an excellent retentive memory may wish to ignore steps 7 and 8 in time, although they will miss the fun of creating their own symbolic code.

If you are artistic and can produce beautiful and imaginative symbols, you may wish to illumine your handiwork with colour and/or calligraphy. Such a piece of work could become a charming greeting card or a framed gift for a friend.

Step 8: Recall the selection using your code

Bring your first code symbol into mental focus and try to recite the part of your selection represented by this symbol. If you are successful, continue on to the next symbol and follow this pattern as far as you can go with accurate recall.

At first this may not be very far but do not be discouraged. Memorization is a faculty which improves with practice.

Step 9: Refer to the text to check for accuracy

This step can be used as needed in conjunction with step 8. Whenever you cannot remember a portion of the text or a word – or you are not sure whether you are quoting correctly from memory – refer immediately back to the text and check for accuracy. Do this as many times as you need to until you establish perfect recall.

When you need a little encouragement, remember that the Báb promised us a wondrous award for our achievement:

> . . . and every breast which committeth His Words to memory, God shall cause, if it were that of a believer, to be filled with His love . . .[12]

Step 10: Recite your selection every day using code or text as necessary

With this step we are imbuing the creative Word with the power of sound and speech:

> Intone, O My servant, the verses of God that have been received by thee, as intoned by them who have drawn nigh unto Him, that the sweetness of thy melody may kindle thine own soul, and attract the hearts of all men. Whoso reciteth, in the privacy of his cham-

> ber, the verses revealed by God, the scattering angels of the Almighty shall scatter abroad the fragrance of the words uttered by his mouth, and shall cause the heart of every righteous man to throb. Though he may, at first, remain unaware of its effect, yet the virtue of the grace vouchsafed unto him must needs sooner or later exercise its influence upon his soul.
>
> *Bahá'u'lláh*[13]

As you recite your verse, be aware of the sound of your voice. Are you intoning the words or merely saying them? Is your voice pleasing to the ear? Check on your tone and inflection. If you feel you need some help, ask a friend to listen and work with you for a while. Have confidence in your ability to be a vehicle for the creative Word.

When you have mastered the memorization and recitation of your verse, you may wish to consider some creative possibilities.

Some of the Persian friends are adept at chanting verses from the writings and it is a joy to listen to them. You may wish to try chanting your verse in your own language.

If you have musical ability, why not attempt to set your verse to music? You may wish to listen to recordings such as *Songs of the Ancient Beauty* or *O Most Mighty Ocean* for inspiration. In this endeavour you have 'Abdu'l-Bahá's full encouragement:

> Try, if thou canst, to use spiritual melodies, songs and tunes, and to bring the earthly music into harmony with the celestial melody. Then thou wilt notice what a great influence music hath and what heavenly joy and life it conferreth. Strike up such a melody and

tune as to cause the nightingales of divine mysteries to be filled with joy and ecstasy.[14]

Utilization

> If they arise to teach My Cause, they must let the breath of Him Who is the Unconstrained, stir them and must spread it abroad on the earth with high resolve, with minds that are wholly centred in Him, and with hearts that are completely detached from and independent of all things, and with souls that are sanctified from the world and its vanities. It behoveth them to choose as the best provision for their journey reliance upon God, and to clothe themselves with the love of their Lord, the Most Exalted, the All-Glorious. If they do so, their words shall influence their hearers. *Bahá'u'lláh*[15]

Step 11: Find as many ways as you can to incorporate the creative Word into your daily conversation at gatherings, firesides, teaching events, lectures, etc.

This step is designed to bring the creative Word out into the world through your daily life and contacts, as the Blessed Beauty advises us in these loving words:

> Consort with all men, O people of Bahá, in a spirit of friendliness and fellowship. If ye be aware of a certain truth, if ye possess a jewel, of which others are deprived, share it with them in a language of utmost kindliness and good-will. If it be accepted, if it fulfil its purpose, your object is attained. If any one should refuse it, leave him unto himself, and beseech God to guide him. Beware lest ye deal unkindly with him. A kindly tongue is the lodestone of the hearts of men.

> It is the bread of the spirit, it clotheth the words with meaning, it is the fountain of the light of wisdom and understanding.[16]

Step 12: Deepen continually on the creative Word. Through meditation and contemplation strive to make these words a living and creative part of yourself.

This step encourages deep meditation, contemplation and reflection on the creative Word, which should form a basis for all the other steps of your life.

Shoghi Effendi has given us some wonderful help with this step.

> When a person becomes a Bahá'í . . . the seed of the spirit starts to grow in the human soul. This seed must be watered by the outpourings of the Holy Spirit. These gifts of the spirit are received through prayer, meditation, study of the Holy Utterances and service to the Cause of God . . .[17]

The National Teaching Committee of the United States commented:

> This makes it clear that studying the Word of God alone is not sufficient; that deepening is really a combination of activities that include prayer, meditation, study, and service. The Guardian placed great emphasis on the notion that reflection must be accompanied by action, stating that to be successful in our efforts for the Cause of God we must 'meditate on the teachings, pray fervently for divine confirmations . . . study the teachings . . . and then act, and above all persevere in action'.

Deepening should be undertaken by individuals on their own, and also by groups of the friends in the context of community life. When Bahá'ís succeed in doing this, marvellous benefits result:

'Hold meetings and read and chant the heavenly teachings, so that city may be illumined with the light of reality and that country become a veritable paradise by the strength of the Holy Spirit . . .'[18]

2

One God

No God is there but Him, the One, the Peerless, the Powerful, the Mighty, the Beneficent. *Bahá'u'lláh*[1]

The purpose of the one true God, exalted be His glory, hath been to bring forth the Mystic Gems out of the mine of man . . . *Bahá'u'lláh*[2]

I am, O my Lord, Thy servant and the son of Thy servant. I bear witness unto Thy unity, and Thy oneness, and to the sanctity of Thy self and the purity of Thine Essence. *Bahá'u'lláh*[3]

No God is there but Thee, the Most Powerful, the Most Exalted, the Help in Peril, the Most Great, the One Being, the Incomparable, the All-Glorious, the Unrestrained. *Bahá'u'lláh*[4]

O God, my God! I bear witness to Thy unity and Thy oneness, and that Thou art God, and that there is none other God but Thee. *Bahá'u'lláh*[5]

Verily Thou art God; there is none other God but Thee! From everlasting Thou wast sanctified from the mention of Thy servants, and exalted above the description of Thy creatures. *Bahá'u'lláh*[6]

'I turn my face to Him Who hath created the Heavens and the earth . . . I am not one of those who add gods to God.' *Quoted by Bahá'u'lláh*[7]

. . . We bear witness unto that whereunto God hath Himself borne witness ere the creation of the heavens and of the earth, that there is none other God but Him, the Almighty, the All-Bounteous. We testify that He is One in His Essence, One in His Attributes. He hath none to equal Him in the whole universe, nor any partner in all creation. *Bahá'u'lláh*[8]

Thou seest me turning towards Thee, holding fast unto the cord of Thy bounty, clinging to the hem of Thy generosity, acknowledging the sanctity of Thy Self and the purity of Thine Essence, and testifying to Thy unity and Thy oneness. *Bahá'u'lláh*[9]

God testifieth to the unity of His Godhood and to the singleness of His own Being. On the throne of eternity, from the inaccessible heights of His station, His tongue proclaimeth that there is none other God but Him. He Himself, independently of all else, hath ever been a witness unto His own oneness, the revealer of His own nature, the glorifier of His own essence. He, verily, is the All-Powerful, the Almighty, the Beauteous.

Bahá'u'lláh[10]

No God is there but Thee, the God of strength, of glory and wisdom. *Bahá'u'lláh*[11]

God testifieth that there is none other God but Him and that He Who hath come from the heaven of divine revelation is the Hidden Secret, the Impenetrable Mystery, Whose advent hath been foretold in the Book of God and hath been heralded by His Prophets and Messengers. *Bahá'u'lláh*[12]

Assist Thou Thy servants, O my Lord, to recognize Thy unity and to declare Thy oneness, that all may gather together around what Thou didst desire in this Day whereon the sun of Thine essence hath shone forth above the horizon of Thy will, and the moon of Thine own being hath risen from the Day-Spring of Thy behest. *Bahá'u'lláh*[13]

O God, Who art the Author of all Manifestations, the Source of all Sources, the Fountain-Head of all Revelations, and the Well-Spring of all Lights! I testify that by Thy Name the heaven of understanding hath been adorned, and the ocean of utterance hath surged, and the dispensations of Thy providence have been promulgated unto the followers of all religions. *Bahá'u'lláh*[14]

I am he, O my God, who testifieth to Thy unity, who acknowledgeth Thy oneness, who boweth humbly before the revelation of Thy majesty, and who recognizeth with downcast countenance the splendours of the light of Thy transcendent glory. *Bahá'u'lláh*[15]

I recognize that there is none other God but Thee, that Thou hast no peer nor partner, none to equal or rival Thee. In Thine unapproachable loftiness Thou hast, from eternity, been exalted above the praise of any one but Thee, and shalt continue for ever, in Thy transcendent singleness and glory, to be sanctified from the glorification of any one except Thine own Self.

Bahá'u'lláh[16]

Glorified art Thou, O Lord my God! My tongue, both the tongue of my body and the tongue of my heart, my limbs and members, every pulsating vein within me, every hair of my head, all proclaim that Thou art God, and that there is none other God beside Thee. From everlasting Thou hast been immeasurably exalted above all similitudes and comparisons, and sanctified from whatsoever pertaineth to the creation Thou hast created and fashioned. From eternity Thou hast been alone, with none to share the majesty of Thy singleness, and hast remained far above the changes and chances to which all Thy creatures are subjected. *Bahá'u'lláh*[17]

No God is there but Thee, the Inaccessible, the All-Glorious, the Most Great. *Bahá'u'lláh*[18]

No God is there beside Thee, the Almighty, the Help in Peril, the All-Glorious, the Most Powerful.

Bahá'u'lláh[19]

Potent art Thou to do what Thou willest, and to rule as Thou pleasest. There is no God but Thee, the God of glory and wisdom. *Bahá'u'lláh*[20]

My God, Whom I worship and adore! I bear witness unto Thy unity and Thy oneness and acknowledge Thy gifts, both in the past and in the present.

Bahá'u'lláh[21]

. . . Thou art One in Thine own Self, one in Thy Cause, and one in Thy Revelation. *Bahá'u'lláh*[22]

All glory be to Thee, O Lord my God! I bear witness for Thee to that whereunto Thou Thyself didst bear witness for Thine own Self, ere the day Thou hadst created the creation or made mention thereof, that Thou art God, and there is none other God beside Thee. From eternity Thou hast, in Thy transcendent oneness, been immeasurably exalted above Thy servants' conception of Thy unity, and wilt to eternity remain, in Thine unapproachable singleness, far above the praise of Thy creatures.

Bahá'u'lláh[23]

Existence itself testifieth to its non-existence when face to face with the manifold revelations of Thy transcendent oneness, and every created thing confesseth, by its very nature, its nothingness when compared with the sacred splendours of the light of Thy unity.

Bahá'u'lláh[24]

Unto Thee be praise, O Lord my God! I testify that Thou art God, and that there is none other God besides Thee. Thou hast from eternity been immeasurably exalted above the praise of any one except Thee, and far above the description of any of Thy creatures. All created things have borne witness to Thy unity, and every dweller in Thy kingdom hath confessed Thy oneness. *Bahá'u'lláh*[25]

Where can separation from Thee be found, O my God, so that reunion with Thee may be clearly recognized at the appearance of the Light of Thy unity, and the revelation of the splendours of the Sun of Thy oneness? *Bahá'u'lláh*[26]

All this hast Thou set down through Thine all-encompassing sovereignty, and apprehended through Thine omnipotent supremacy. *Bahá'u'lláh*[27]

Through that Word the realities of all created things were shaken, were divided, separated, scattered, combined and reunited, disclosing, in both the contingent world and the heavenly kingdom, entities of a new creation, and revealing, in the unseen realms, the signs and tokens of Thy unity and oneness. *Bahá'u'lláh*[28]

Were any one except Thee to be deemed worthy of mention, in all the kingdoms of Thy creation, from the highest realms of immortality down to the level of this nether world, how could it, then, be demonstrated that Thou art established upon the throne of Thy unity, and how could the wondrous virtues of Thy oneness and Thy singleness be glorified? *Bahá'u'lláh*[29]

Since Thou hast, O my God, established Thyself upon the throne of Thy transcendent unity, and ascended the mercy seat of Thy oneness, it befitteth Thee to blot out from the hearts of all beings whatsoever may keep them back from gaining admittance into the sanctuary of Thy Divine mysteries, and may shut them out from the tabernacle of Thy Divinity, that all hearts may mirror Thy beauty, and may reveal Thee, and speak of Thee, and that all created things may show forth the tokens of Thy most august sovereignty, and shed the splendours of the light of Thy most holy governance, and that all who are in heaven and on earth may laud and magnify Thy unity, and give Thee glory, for having manifested Thy Self unto them through Him Who is the Revealer of Thy oneness. *Bahá'u'lláh*[30]

I bear witness, this very moment, to what Thou hath testified for Thine own Self, ere Thou hadst created the heavens and the earth, that Thou art God, and that there is none other God besides Thee. *Bahá'u'lláh*[31]

No one besides Thee hath ever been found worthy to be mentioned before the Tabernacle of Thy unity, and none except Thyself hath proved himself capable of being praised within the hallowed court of Thy oneness. *Bahá'u'lláh*[32]

They have strayed so far from Thee that should any of Thy loved ones deliver unto them the wondrous tokens of Thy unity, and the gem-like utterances that attest Thy transcendent oneness, they would thrust their fingers into their ears, and would cavil at him and mock him. *Bahá'u'lláh*[33]

All praise be to the one true God – exalted be His glory – inasmuch as He hath, through the Pen of the Most High, unlocked the doors of men's hearts.

Bahá'u'lláh[34]

. . . know thou that We bear witness unto that whereunto God hath Himself borne witness ere the creation of the heavens and of the earth, that there is none other God but Him, the Almighty, the All-Bounteous. We testify that He is One in His Essence, One in His attributes. He hath none to equal Him in the whole universe, nor any partner in all creation. He hath sent forth His Messengers, and sent down His Books, that they may announce unto His creatures the Straight Path.

Bahá'u'lláh[35]

O Lord! The tongue of my tongue and the heart of my heart and the spirit of my spirit and my outward and inmost beings bear witness to Thy unity and Thy oneness, Thy power and Thine omnipotence, Thy grandeur and Thy sovereignty, and attest Thy glory, loftiness and authority. I testify that Thou art God and that there is none other God besides Thee. *Bahá'u'lláh*[36]

3

Oneness of Humankind

Ye are the fruits of one tree, and the leaves of one branch. Deal ye with one another with the utmost love and harmony, with friendliness and fellowship.

Bahá'u'lláh[1]

So powerful is the light of unity that it can illuminate the whole earth. *Bahá'u'lláh*[2]

Consort with all men, O people of Bahá, in a spirit of friendliness and fellowship. *Bahá'u'lláh*[3]

Through Him the light of unity hath shone forth above the horizon of the world, and the law of oneness hath been revealed amidst the nations . . . *Bahá'u'lláh*[4]

That one indeed is a man who, today, dedicateth himself to the service of the entire human race.

Bahá'u'lláh[5]

Furthermore, how numerous are those peoples of divers beliefs, of conflicting creeds, and opposing temperaments, who, through the reviving fragrance of the Divine springtime, breathing from the Riḍván of God, have been arrayed with the new robe of divine Unity, and have drunk from the cup of His singleness!

Bahá'u'lláh[6]

Justice and equity are twin Guardians that watch over men. From them are revealed such blessed and perspicuous words as are the cause of the well-being of the world and the protection of the nations. *Bahá'u'lláh*[7]

We, verily, have come to unite and weld together all that dwell on earth. *Bahá'u'lláh*[8]

He Who is the Lord of Being is witness that this Wronged One hath besought from God for His creatures whatever is conducive to unity and harmony, fellowship and concord. *Bahá'u'lláh*[9]

This is the day whereon all peoples should shed the light of unity and concord. *Bahá'u'lláh*[10]

It is not his to boast who loveth his country, but it is his who loveth the world. *Bahá'u'lláh*[11]

Be ye as the fingers of one hand, the members of one body. *Bahá'u'lláh*[12]

He Who is your Lord, the All-Merciful, cherisheth in His heart the desire of beholding the entire human race as one soul and one body. *Bahá'u'lláh*[13]

How resplendent the luminaries of knowledge that shine in an atom, and how vast the oceans of wisdom that surge within a drop! To a supreme degree is this true of man, who, among all created things, hath been invested with the robe of such gifts, and hath been singled out for the glory of such distinction. For in him are potentially revealed all the attributes and names of God to a degree that no other created being hath excelled or surpassed. *Bahá'u'lláh*[14]

For the highest and most excelling grace bestowed upon men is the grace of 'attaining unto the Presence of God' and of His recognition, which has been promised unto all people. *Bahá'u'lláh*[15]

The incomparable Creator hath created all men from one same substance, and hath exalted their reality above the rest of His creatures. *Bahá'u'lláh*[16]

It is not for him to pride himself who loveth his own country, but rather for him who loveth the whole world. The earth is but one country, and mankind its citizens. *Bahá'u'lláh*[17]

That which the Lord hath ordained as the sovereign remedy and mightiest instrument for the healing of all the world is the union of all its peoples in one universal Cause, one common Faith. *Bahá'u'lláh*[18]

Ye dwell in one world, and have been created through the operation of one Will. Blessed is he who mingleth with all men in a spirit of utmost kindliness and love. *Bahá'u'lláh*[19]

If any man were to meditate on that which the Scriptures, sent down from the heaven of God's holy Will, have revealed, he will readily recognize that their purpose is that all men shall be regarded as one soul, so that the seal bearing the words 'The Kingdom shall be God's' may be stamped on every heart, and the light of Divine bounty, of grace, and mercy may envelop all mankind.

Bahá'u'lláh[20]

Likewise reflect upon the perfection of man's creation, and that all these planes and states are folded up and hidden away within him.

> Dost thou reckon thyself only a puny form
> When within thee the universe is folded?

Bahá'u'lláh[21]

Ye are all the leaves of one tree and the drops of one ocean.

Bahá'u'lláh[22]

The fruits of the tree of man have ever been and are goodly deeds and a praiseworthy character.

Bahá'u'lláh[23]

4

Independent Investigation of Truth

Only when the lamp of search, of earnest striving, of longing desire, of passionate devotion . . . is kindled within the seeker's heart . . . will the darkness of error be dispelled, the mists of doubts and misgivings be dissipated, and the lights of knowledge and certitude envelop his being. *Bahá'u'lláh*[1]

Blessed is the believer who hath in this Day embraced the Truth and the man of fixed resolve whom the hosts of tyranny have been powerless to affright.

Bahá'u'lláh[2]

So great shall be the discernment of this seeker that he will discriminate between truth and falsehood, even as he doth distinguish the sun from shadow.

Bahá'u'lláh[3]

What 'oppression' is more grievous than that a soul seeking the truth, and wishing to attain unto the knowledge of God, should know not where to go for it and from whom to seek it? *Bahá'u'lláh*[4]

Cleave to the Root of Knowledge, and to Him Who is the Fountain thereof, that thou mayest find thyself independent of all who claim to be well versed in human learning, and whose claim no clear proof, nor the testimony of any enlightening book, can support.

Bahá'u'lláh[5]

He should not hesitate to offer up his life for his Beloved, nor allow the censure of the people to turn him away from the Truth. *Bahá'u'lláh*[6]

Hear Me, ye mortal birds! In the Rose Garden of changeless splendour a Flower hath begun to bloom, compared to which every other flower is but a thorn, and before the brightness of Whose glory the very essence of beauty must pale and wither. Arise, therefore, and, with the whole enthusiasm of your hearts, with all the eagerness of your souls, the full fervour of your will, and the concentrated efforts of your entire being, strive to attain the paradise of His presence, and endeavour to inhale the fragrance of the incorruptible Flower, to breathe the sweet savours of holiness, and to obtain a portion of this perfume of celestial glory.

Bahá'u'lláh[7]

Let the flame of search burn with such fierceness within your hearts as to enable you to attain your supreme and most exalted goal – the station at which ye can draw nigh unto, and be united with, your Best-Beloved.

Bahá'u'lláh[8]

. . . man can never hope to attain unto the knowledge of the All-Glorious, can never quaff from the stream of divine knowledge and wisdom, can never enter the abode of immortality, nor partake of the cup of divine nearness and favour, unless and until he ceases to regard the words and deeds of mortal men as a standard for the true understanding and recognition of God and His Prophets. *Bahá'u'lláh*[9]

They whose sight is keen, whose ears are retentive, whose hearts are enlightened, and whose breasts are dilated, recognize both truth and falsehood, and distinguish the one from the other. *Bahá'u'lláh*[10]

Would that the hearts of men could be cleansed from these man-made limitations and obscure thoughts imposed upon them! haply they may be illumined by the light of the Sun of true knowledge, and comprehend the mysteries of divine wisdom. *Bahá'u'lláh*[11]

Not, however, until thou consumest with the flame of utter detachment those veils of idle learning, that are current amongst men, canst thou behold the resplendent morn of true knowledge. *Bahá'u'lláh*[12]

It is for thee to direct thyself towards the Ultimate Goal, and the Supreme End, and the Most Sublime Pinnacle, that thou mayest hear and behold what hath been revealed by God, the Lord of the worlds. *Bahá'u'lláh*[13]

O concourse of the fair-minded! Observe and reflect upon the billows of the ocean of the utterance and knowledge of God, so that ye may testify with your inner and outer tongues that with Him is the knowledge of all that is in the Book. *Bahá'u'lláh*[14]

Open Thou, O my Lord, mine eyes and the eyes of all them that have sought Thee, that we may recognize Thee with Thine own eyes. *Bahá'u'lláh*[15]

Aside from these things, scrutinize the Writings with thine own eyes and ponder upon that which hath come to pass. *Bahá'u'lláh*[16]

5

The Common Foundation of All Religions

That the divers communions of the earth, and the manifold systems of religious belief, should never be allowed to foster the feelings of animosity among men, is, in this Day, of the essence of the Faith of God and His Religion. These principles and laws, these firmly-established and mighty systems, have proceeded from one Source, and are rays of one Light. That they differ one from another is to be attributed to the varying requirements of the ages in which they were promulgated. *Bahá'u'lláh*[1]

In truth, religion is a radiant light and an impregnable stronghold for the protection and welfare of the peoples of the world . . . *Bahá'u'lláh*[2]

Religion is, verily, the chief instrument for the establishment of order in the world, and of tranquillity amongst its peoples. *Bahá'u'lláh*[3]

The Prophets and Messengers of God have been sent down for the sole purpose of guiding mankind to the straight Path of Truth. *Bahá'u'lláh*[4]

The Great Being saith: O ye children of men! The fundamental purpose animating the Faith of God and His Religion is to safeguard the interests and promote the unity of the human race, and to foster the spirit of love and fellowship amongst men. Suffer it not to become a source of dissension and discord, of hate and enmity. This is the straight Path, the fixed and immovable foundation. Whatever is raised on this foundation, the changes and chances of the world can never impair its strength, nor will the revolution of countless centuries undermine its structure. Our hope is that the world's religious leaders and the rulers thereof will unitedly arise for the reformation of this age and the rehabilitation of its fortunes. *Bahá'u'lláh*[5]

O people! Consort with the followers of all religions in a spirit of friendliness and fellowship. *Bahá'u'lláh*[6]

The purpose of religion as revealed from the heaven of God's holy Will is to establish unity and concord amongst the peoples of the world; make it not the cause of dissension and strife. The religion of God and His divine law are the most potent instruments and the surest of all means for the dawning of the light of unity amongst men. *Bahá'u'lláh*[7]

Even as He hath revealed: 'No distinction do We make between any of His Messengers!' For they one and all summon the people of the earth to acknowledge the Unity of God, and herald unto them the Kawthar of an infinite grace and bounty. *Bahá'u'lláh*[8]

They are all invested with the robe of Prophethood, and honoured with the mantle of glory. Thus hath Muḥammad, the Point of the Qur'án, revealed: 'I am all the Prophets.' Likewise, He saith: 'I am the first Adam, Noah, Moses, and Jesus.' *Bahá'u'lláh*[9]

Sayings such as this, which indicate the essential unity of those Exponents of Oneness, have also emanated from the Channels of God's immortal utterance, and the Treasuries of the gems of divine knowledge, and have been recorded in the scriptures. *Bahá'u'lláh*[10]

These Countenances are the recipients of the Divine Command, and the day-springs of His Revelation. This Revelation is exalted above the veils of plurality and the exigencies of number. Thus He saith: 'Our Cause is but one.' *Bahá'u'lláh*[11]

It is clear and evident to thee that all the Prophets are the Temples of the Cause of God, Who have appeared clothed in divers attire. *Bahá'u'lláh*[12]

Say: O leaders of religion! Weigh not the Book of God with such standards and sciences as are current amongst you, for the Book itself is the unerring Balance established amongst men. *Bahá'u'lláh*[13]

Consort with all religions with amity and concord, that they may inhale from you the sweet fragrance of God.

Bahá'u'lláh[14]

This is the changeless Faith of God, eternal in the past, eternal in the future. *Bahá'u'lláh*[15]

The second Ṭaráz is to consort with the followers of all religions in a spirit of friendliness and fellowship, to proclaim that which the Speaker on Sinai hath set forth and to observe fairness in all matters. *Bahá'u'lláh*[16]

6

The Essential Harmony of Science and Religion

Such things have appeared in this Revelation that there is no recourse for either the exponents of science and knowledge or the manifestations of justice and equity other than to recognize them. *Bahá'u'lláh*[1]

. . . every created thing will, according to its capacity and limitations, be invested with the power to unfold the knowledge of the most marvellous sciences, and will be empowered to manifest them in the course of time at the bidding of Him Who is the Almighty, the All-Knowing. *Bahá'u'lláh*[2]

Such arts and sciences, however, as are productive of good results, and bring forth their fruit, and are conducive to the well-being and tranquillity of men have been, and will remain, acceptable before God. *Bahá'u'lláh*[3]

The third Tajallí is concerning arts, crafts and sciences. Knowledge is as wings to man's life, and a ladder for his ascent. Its acquisition is incumbent upon everyone. The knowledge of such sciences, however, should be acquired as can profit the peoples of the earth, and not those which begin with words and end with words. Great indeed is the claim of scientists and craftsmen on the peoples of the world. Unto this beareth witness the Mother Book on the day of His return. *Bahá'u'lláh*[4]

Should the Will of God assist Us, there would flow out from the Pen of the Divine Expounder a lengthy exposition of that which hath been mentioned, and there would be revealed, in the field of arts and sciences, what would renew the world and the nations. *Bahá'u'lláh*[5]

The eleventh Glad-Tidings: It is permissible to study sciences and arts, but such sciences as are useful and would redound to the progress and advancement of the people. Thus hath it been decreed by Him Who is the Ordainer, the All-Wise. *Bahá'u'lláh*[6]

O people of Bahá! The source of crafts, sciences and arts is the power of reflection. Make ye every effort that out of this ideal mine there may gleam forth such pearls of wisdom and utterance as will promote the well-being and harmony of all the kindreds of the earth.

Bahá'u'lláh[7]

. . . religion must reconcile and be in harmony with science and reason. If the religious beliefs of mankind are contrary to science and opposed to reason, they are none other than superstitions and without divine authority, for the Lord God has endowed man with the faculty of reason in order that through its exercise he may arrive at the verities of existence. *'Abdu'l-Bahá*[8]

If religion were in harmony with science and they walked together, much of the hatred and bitterness now bringing misery to the human race would be at an end.

'Abdu'l-Bahá[9]

Put all your beliefs into harmony with science; there can be no opposition, for truth is one. When religion, shorn of its superstitions, traditions, and unintelligent dogmas, shows its conformity with science, then will there be a great unifying, cleansing force in the world which will sweep before it all wars, disagreements, discords and struggles – and then will mankind be united in the power of the Love of God. *'Abdu'l-Bahá*[10]

If religion is opposed to reason and science, faith is impossible; and when faith and confidence in the divine religion are not manifest in the heart, there can be no spiritual attainment. *'Abdu'l-Bahá*[11]

7

Equality of Women and Men

Exalted, immensely exalted is He Who hath removed differences and established harmony. Glorified, infinitely glorified is He Who hath caused discord to cease, and decreed solidarity and unity. Praised be God, the Pen of the Most High hath lifted distinctions from between His servants and handmaidens, and through His consummate favours and all-encompassing mercy, hath conferred upon all a station and rank on the same plane. *Bahá'u'lláh*[1]

O My handmaiden, O My leaf! Render thou thanks unto the Best-Beloved of the world for having attained this boundless grace at a time when the world's learned and most distinguished men have remained deprived thereof. *Bahá'u'lláh*[2]

In this Day the Hand of divine grace hath removed all distinctions. The servants of God and His handmaidens are regarded on the same plane. Blessed is the servant who hath attained unto that which God hath decreed, and likewise the leaf moving in accordance with the breezes of His will. This favour is great and this station lofty. His bounties and bestowals are ever present and manifest. Who is able to offer befitting gratitude for His successive bestowals and continuous favours?

Bahá'u'lláh[3]

By My Life! The names of handmaidens who are devoted to God are written and set down by the Pen of the Most High in the Crimson Book. They excel over men in the sight of God. How numerous are the heroes and knights in the field who are bereft of the True One and have no share in His recognition, but thou hast attained and received thy fill. *Bahá'u'lláh*[4]

Verily the Pen of the Most High hath borne witness unto thy recognition of Him, thy love for Him and thy turning towards the Ancient Countenance at a time when the world hath rejected Him, save those whom God, the Most High, hath willed . . .

Well is it with thee for having adorned thyself with the ornament of the love of God and for having been enabled to make mention of Him and utter His praise. Divine grace, in its entirety, is in the mighty grasp of God, exalted be He. He conferreth it upon whomsoever He willeth. How many a man considered himself a celebrated divine and a repository of heavenly mysteries, and yet when the slightest test visited him, he arose with such opposition and denial as to cause the Concourse on High to moan and lament. Through the bestowals of the Lord, however, and His infinite favour, thou hast attained unto the hidden secret and the well-guarded treasure. Preserve then, in the name of God, this lofty station and conceal it from the eyes of betrayers. The glory shining from the horizon of My Kingdom be upon thee and upon every handmaiden who hath attained the splendours of My sublime Throne.

Bahá'u'lláh[5]

The world of humanity has two wings, as it were: One is the female; the other is the male. If one wing be defective, the strong perfect wing will not be capable of flight. The world of humanity has two hands. If one be imperfect, the capable hand is restricted and unable to perform its duties. *'Abdu'l-Bahá*[6]

The happiness of mankind will be realized when women and men coordinate and advance equally, for each is the complement and helpmeet of the other.

'Abdu'l-Bahá[7]

Women and men have been and will always be equal in the sight of God. The Dawning-Place of the Light of God sheddeth its radiance upon all with the same effulgence. Verily God created women for men, and men for women. The most beloved of people before God are the most steadfast and those who have surpassed others in their love for God, exalted be His glory . . .

'Abdu'l-Bahá[8]

8

Elimination of Prejudices of All Kinds

That the divers communions of the earth, and the manifold systems of religious belief, should never be allowed to foster the feelings of animosity among men, is, in this Day, of the essence of the Faith of God and His Religion. *Bahá'u'lláh*[1]

A kindly tongue is the lodestone of the hearts of men. It is the bread of the spirit, it clotheth the words with meaning, it is the fountain of the light of wisdom and understanding . . . *Bahá'u'lláh*[2]

O contending peoples and kindreds of the earth! Set your faces towards unity, and let the radiance of its light shine upon you. Gather ye together, and for the sake of God resolve to root out whatever is the source of contention amongst you. Then will the effulgence of the worlds' great Luminary envelop the whole earth, and its inhabitants become the citizens of one city, and the occupants of one and the same throne. *Bahá'u'lláh*[3]

Religious fanaticism and hatred are a world-devouring fire, whose violence none can quench. The Hand of Divine power can, alone, deliver mankind from this desolating affliction. *Bahá'u'lláh*[4]

There can be no doubt whatever that the peoples of the world, of whatever race or religion, derive their inspiration from one heavenly Source, and are the subjects of one God. *Bahá'u'lláh*[5]

Gird up the loins of your endeavour, O people of Bahá, that haply the tumult of religious dissension and strife that agitateth the peoples of the earth may be stilled, that every trace of it may be completely obliterated.

Bahá'u'lláh[6]

Revile ye not one another. We, verily, have come to unite and weld together all that dwell on earth.

Bahá'u'lláh[7]

We, verily, have chosen courtesy, and made it the true mark of such as are nigh unto Him. Courtesy is, in truth, a raiment which fitteth all men, whether young or old. *Bahá'u'lláh*[8]

The most glorious fruit of the tree of knowledge is this exalted word: Of one tree are all ye the fruit, and of one bough the leaves. Let not man glory in this that he loveth his country, let him rather glory in this that he loveth his kind. *Bahá'u'lláh*[9]

Beware lest the desires of the flesh and of a corrupt inclination provoke divisions among you. Be ye as the fingers of one hand, the members of one body.

Bahá'u'lláh[10]

O Son of Being! How couldst thou forget thine own faults and busy thyself with the faults of others? Whoso doeth this is accursed of Me. *Bahá'u'lláh*[11]

O Son of Man! Breathe not the sins of others so long as thou art thyself a sinner. Shouldst thou transgress this command, accursed wouldst thou be, and to this I bear witness. *Bahá'u'lláh*[12]

O My Servant! Purge thy heart from malice and, innocent of envy, enter the divine court of holiness.

Bahá'u'lláh[13]

O Children of Men! Know ye not why We created you all from the same dust? That no one should exalt himself over the other. Ponder at all times in your hearts how ye were created. Since We have created you all from one same substance it is incumbent on you to be even as one soul, to walk with the same feet, eat with the same mouth and dwell in the same land, that from your inmost being, by your deeds and actions, the signs of oneness and the essence of detachment may be made manifest. Such is My counsel to you, O concourse of light! Heed ye this counsel that ye may obtain the fruit of holiness from the tree of wondrous glory.

Bahá'u'lláh[14]

O Son of Dust! Verily I say unto thee: Of all men the most negligent is he that disputeth idly and seeketh to advance himself over his brother. Say, O brethren! Let deeds, not words, be your adorning. *Bahá'u'lláh*[15]

O Children of Desire! Put away the garment of vainglory, and divest yourselves of the attire of haughtiness. *Bahá'u'lláh*[16]

O ye that dwell on earth! The distinguishing feature that marketh the pre-eminent character of this Supreme Revelation consisteth in that We have, on the one hand, blotted out from the pages of God's holy Book whatsoever hath been the cause of strife, of malice and mischief amongst the children of men, and have, on the other, laid down the essential prerequisites of concord, of understanding, of complete and enduring unity. Well is it with them that keep My statutes. *Bahá'u'lláh*[17]

No one truth can contradict another truth. Light is good in whatsoever lamp it is burning! A rose is beautiful in whatsoever garden it may bloom! A star has the same radiance if it shines from the East or from the West. Be free from prejudice, so will you love the Sun of Truth from whatsoever point in the horizon it may arise! *'Abdu'l-Bahá*[18]

9

Universal Compulsory Education

Man is the supreme Talisman. Lack of a proper education hath, however, deprived him of that which he doth inherently possess. *Bahá'u'lláh*[1]

The Great Being saith: Regard man as a mine rich in gems of inestimable value. Education can, alone, cause it to reveal its treasures, and enable mankind to benefit therefrom. *Bahá'u'lláh*[2]

The Pen of Glory counselleth everyone regarding the instruction and education of children. Behold that which the Will of God hath revealed upon Our arrival in the Prison City and recorded in the Most Holy Book. Unto every father hath been enjoined the instruction of his son and daughter in the art of reading and writing and in all that hath been laid down in the Holy Tablet. He that putteth away that which is commanded unto him, the Trustees are then to take from him that which is required for their instruction, if he be wealthy, and if not the matter devolveth upon the House of Justice. *Bahá'u'lláh*[3]

Bend your energies to whatever may foster the education of men. *Bahá'u'lláh*[4]

From the heaven of God's Will, and for the purpose of ennobling the world of being and of elevating the minds and souls of men, hath been sent down that which is the most effective instrument for the education of the whole human race. *Bahá'u'lláh*[5]

Address yourselves to the promotion of the well-being and tranquillity of the children of men. Bend your minds and wills to the education of the peoples and kindreds of the earth, that haply the dissensions that divide it may, through the power of the Most Great Name, be blotted out from its face, and all mankind become the upholders of one Order, and the inhabitants of one City. *Bahá'u'lláh*[6]

It is incumbent upon everyone to firmly adhere to and observe that which hath streamed forth from Our Most Exalted Pen. God, the True One, beareth Me witness, and every atom in existence is moved to testify that such means as lead to the elevation, the advancement, the education, the protection and the regeneration of the peoples of the earth have been clearly set forth by Us and are revealed in the Holy Books and Tablets by the Pen of Glory. *Bahá'u'lláh*[7]

Everyone, whether man or woman, should hand over to a trusted person a portion of what he or she earneth through trade, agriculture or other occupation, for the training and education of children, to be spent for this purpose with the knowledge of the Trustees of the House of Justice. *Bahá'u'lláh*[8]

In truth, knowledge is a veritable treasure for man, and a source of glory, of bounty, of joy, of exaltation, of cheer and gladness unto him. Thus hath the Tongue of Grandeur spoken in this most Great Prison.

Bahá'u'lláh[9]

Consider, for instance, the revelation of the light of the Name of God, the Educator. Behold, how in all things the evidences of such a revelation are manifest, how the betterment of all beings dependeth upon it. This education is of two kinds. The one is universal. Its influence pervadeth all things and sustaineth them. It is for this reason that God hath assumed the title, 'Lord of all worlds.' The other is confined to them that have come under the shadow of this Name, and sought the shelter of this most mighty Revelation. *Bahá'u'lláh*[10]

He that bringeth up his son or the son of another, it is as though he hath brought up a son of Mine; upon him rest My Glory, My Loving-Kindness, My Mercy, that have compassed the world. *Bahá'u'lláh*[11]

10

A Spiritual Solution to the Economic Problem

Be generous in prosperity, and thankful in adversity. Be worthy of the trust of thy neighbour, and look upon him with a bright and friendly face. Be a treasure to the poor, an admonisher to the rich, an answerer of the cry of the needy, a preserver of the sanctity of thy pledge. Be fair in thy judgement, and guarded in thy speech. Be unjust to no man, and show all meekness to all men. Be as a lamp unto them that walk in darkness, a joy to the sorrowful, a sea for the thirsty, a haven for the distressed, an upholder and defender of the victim of oppression. Let integrity and uprightness distinguish all thine acts. Be a home for the stranger, a balm to the suffering, a tower of strength for the fugitive. Be eyes to the blind, and a guiding light unto the feet of the erring. Be an ornament to the countenance of truth, a crown to the brow of fidelity, a pillar of the temple of righteousness, a breath of life to the body of mankind, an ensign of the hosts of justice, a luminary above the horizon of virtue, a dew to the soil of the human heart, an ark on the ocean of knowledge, a sun in the heaven of bounty, a gem on the diadem of wisdom, a shining light in the firmament of thy generation, a fruit upon the tree of humility. *Bahá'u'lláh*[1]

Say: Rejoice not in the things ye possess; tonight they are yours, tomorrow others will possess them. *Bahá'u'lláh*[2]

O My Servant! The best of men are they that earn a livelihood by their calling and spend upon themselves and upon their kindred for the love of God, the Lord of all worlds. *Bahá'u'lláh*[3]

By God, the True One! I am Trustworthiness and the revelation thereof, and the beauty thereof. I will recompense whosoever will cleave unto Me, and recognize My rank and station, and hold fast unto My hem. I am the most great ornament of the people of Bahá, and the vesture of glory unto all who are in the kingdom of creation. I am the supreme instrument for the prosperity of the world, and the horizon of assurance unto all beings. *Bahá'u'lláh*[4]

The fourth Ṭaráz concerneth trustworthiness. Verily it is the door of security for all that dwell on earth and a token of glory on the part of the All-Merciful. He who partaketh thereof hath indeed partaken of the treasures of wealth and prosperity. Trustworthiness is the greatest portal leading unto the tranquillity and security of the people. In truth the stability of every affair hath depended and doth depend upon it. All the domains of power, of grandeur and of wealth are illumined by its light. *Bahá'u'lláh*[5]

Say: O people of God! Adorn your temples with the adornment of trustworthiness and piety. Help, then, your Lord with the hosts of goodly deeds and a praiseworthy character. *Bahá'u'lláh*[6]

Success or failure, gain or loss, must therefore, depend upon man's own exertions. The more he striveth, the greater will be his progress. *Bahá'u'lláh*[7]

We have learned that you are increasing your outlay every year, and are laying the burden thereof on your subjects. This, verily, is more than they can bear, and is a grievous injustice. *Bahá'u'lláh*[8]

Know ye that the poor are the trust of God in your midst. Watch that ye betray not His trust, that ye deal not unjustly with them and that ye walk not in the ways of the treacherous. *Bahá'u'lláh*[9]

O son of man! If thine eyes be turned towards mercy, forsake the things that profit thee, and cleave unto that which will profit mankind. *Bahá'u'lláh*[10]

Lay fast hold on whatever will profit you, and profit the peoples of the world. Thus commandeth you the King of Eternity, Who is manifest in His Most Great Name. *Bahá'u'lláh*[11]

O my friend! In all circumstances one should seize upon every means which will promote security and tranquillity among the peoples of the world. *Bahá'u'lláh*[12]

The first Ṭaráz and the first effulgence which hath dawned from the horizon of the Mother Book is that man should know his own self and recognize that which leadeth unto loftiness or lowliness, glory or abasement, wealth or poverty. Having attained the stage of fulfilment and reached his maturity, man standeth in need of wealth, and such wealth as he acquireth through crafts or professions is commendable and praiseworthy in the estimation of men of wisdom, and especially in the eyes of servants who dedicate themselves to the education of the world and to the edification of its peoples. *Bahá'u'lláh*[13]

Our purpose is that all men may cleave unto that which will reduce unnecessary labour and exertion, so that their days may be befittingly spent and ended.
Bahá'u'lláh[14]

O Son of Spirit! I created thee rich, why dost thou bring thyself down to poverty? Noble I made thee, wherewith dost thou abase thyself? Out of the essence of knowledge I gave thee being, why seekest thou enlightenment from anyone beside Me? Out of the clay of love I moulded thee, how dost thou busy thyself with another? Turn thy sight unto thyself, that thou mayest find Me standing within thee, mighty, powerful and self-subsisting. *Bahá'u'lláh*[15]

O Son of Spirit! Vaunt not thyself over the poor, for I lead him on his way and behold thee in thy evil plight and confound thee for evermore. *Bahá'u'lláh*[16]

O Children of Dust! Tell the rich of the midnight sighing of the poor, lest heedlessness lead them into the path of destruction, and deprive them of the Tree of Wealth. To give and to be generous are attributes of Mine; well is it with him that adorneth himself with My virtues! *Bahá'u'lláh*[17]

O Quintessence of Passion! Put away all covetousness and seek contentment; for the covetous hath ever been deprived, and the contented hath ever been loved and praised. *Bahá'u'lláh*[18]

O Ye that Pride Yourselves on Mortal Riches! Know ye in truth that wealth is a mighty barrier between the seeker and his desire, the lover and his beloved. The rich, but for a few, shall in no wise attain the court of His presence nor enter the city of content and resignation. Well is it then with him, who, being rich, is not hindered by his riches from the eternal kingdom, nor deprived by them of imperishable dominion. By the Most Great Name! The splendour of such a wealthy man shall illuminate the dwellers of heaven even as the sun enlightens the people of the earth! *Bahá'u'lláh*[19]

O Ye Rich Ones on Earth! The poor in your midst are My trust; guard ye My trust, and be not intent only on your own ease. *Bahá'u'lláh*[20]

O My Servants! Ye are the trees of My garden; ye must give forth goodly and wondrous fruits, that ye yourselves and others may profit therefrom. Thus it is incumbent on every one to engage in crafts and professions, for therein lies the secret of wealth, O men of understanding! For results depend upon means, and the grace of God shall be all-sufficient unto you. Trees that yield no fruit have been and will ever be for the fire.

Bahá'u'lláh[21]

Therefore as a token of favour towards men We have prescribed that interest on money should be treated like other business transactions that are current amongst men. Thus, now that this lucid commandment hath descended from the heaven of the Will of God, it is lawful and proper to charge interest on money, that the people of the world may, in a spirit of amity and fellowship and with joy and gladness, devotedly engage themselves in magnifying the Name of Him Who is the Well-Beloved of all mankind. *Bahá'u'lláh*[22]

He hath now made interest on money lawful, even as He had made it unlawful in the past. Within His grasp He holdeth the kingdom of authority.

Bahá'u'lláh[23]

It is incumbent upon the ministers of the House of Justice to promote the Lesser Peace so that the people of the earth may be relieved from the burden of exorbitant expenditures. This matter is imperative and absolutely essential, inasmuch as hostilities and conflict lie at the root of affliction and calamity. *Bahá'u'lláh*[24]

11

A Universal Auxiliary Language

One day, while in Constantinople, Kamál Páshá visited this Wronged One. Our conversation turned upon topics profitable unto man. He said that he had learned several languages. In reply We observed: 'You have wasted your life. It beseemeth you and the other officials of the Government to convene a gathering and choose one of the divers languages, and likewise one of the existing scripts, or else to create a new language and a new script to be taught children in schools throughout the world. They would, in this way, be acquiring only two languages, one their own native tongue, the other the language in which all the peoples of the world would converse. Were men to take fast hold on that which hath been mentioned, the whole earth would come to be regarded as one country, and the people would be relieved and freed from the necessity of acquiring and teaching different languages.' *Bahá'u'lláh*[1]

The sixth Ishráq is union and concord amongst the children of men. From the beginning of time the light of unity hath shed its divine radiance upon the world, and the greatest means for the promotion of that unity is for the peoples of the world to understand one another's writing and speech. In former Epistles We have enjoined upon the Trustees of the House of Justice either to choose one language from among those now existing or to adopt a new one, and in like manner to select a common script, both of which should be taught in all the schools of the world. Thus will the earth be regarded as one country and one home. *Bahá'u'lláh*[2]

Likewise He saith: Among the things which are conducive to unity and concord and will cause the whole earth to be regarded as one country is that the divers languages be reduced to one language and in like manner the scripts used in the world be confined to a single script. It is incumbent upon all nations to appoint some men of understanding and erudition to convene a gathering and through joint consultation choose one language from among the varied existing languages, or create a new one, to be taught to the children in all the schools of the world. *Bahá'u'lláh*[3]

The day is approaching when all the peoples of the world will have adopted one universal language and one common script. When this is achieved, to whatsoever city a man may journey, it shall be as if he were entering his own home. *Bahá'u'lláh*[4]

It behoveth the sovereigns of the world – may God assist them – or the ministers of the earth to take counsel together and to adopt one of the existing languages or a new one to be taught to children in schools throughout the world, and likewise one script. Thus the whole earth will come to be regarded as one country.

Bahá'u'lláh[5]

Languages must be reduced to one common language to be taught in all the schools of the world.

Bahá'u'lláh[6]

We have formerly ordained that people should converse in two languages, yet efforts must be made to reduce them to one, likewise the scripts of the world, that men's lives may not be dissipated and wasted in learning divers languages. Thus the whole earth would come to be regarded as one city and one land. *Bahá'u'lláh*[7]

O members of parliaments throughout the world! Select ye a single language for the use of all on earth, and adopt ye likewise a common script. God, verily, maketh plain for you that which shall profit you and enable you to be independent of others. He, of a truth, is the Most Bountiful, the All-Knowing, the All-Informed. This will be the cause of unity, could ye but comprehend it, and the greatest instrument for promoting harmony and civilization, would that ye might understand! We have appointed two signs for the coming of age of the human race: the first, which is the most firm foundation, We have set down in other of Our Tablets, while the second hath been revealed in this wondrous Book.

Bahá'u'lláh[8]

12

Universal Peace Upheld by a World Government

The well-being of mankind, its peace and security, are unattainable unless and until its unity is firmly established.
Bahá'u'lláh[1]

Lay not aside the fear of God, O kings of the earth, and beware that ye transgress not the bounds which the Almighty hath fixed. Observe the injunctions laid upon you in His Book, and take good heed not to overstep their limits. Be vigilant, that ye may not do injustice to anyone, be it to the extent of a grain of mustard seed. Tread ye the path of justice, for this, verily, is the straight path.

Compose your differences, and reduce your armaments, that the burden of your expenditures may be lightened, and that your minds and hearts may be tranquillized. Heal the dissensions that divide you, and ye will no longer be in need of any armaments except what the protection of your cities and territories demandeth. Fear ye God, and take heed not to outstrip the bounds of moderation, and be numbered among the extravagant.
Bahá'u'lláh[2]

O rulers of the earth! Be reconciled among yourselves, that ye may need no more armaments save in a measure to safeguard your territories and dominions. Beware lest ye disregard the counsel of the All-Knowing, the Faithful. *Bahá'u'lláh*[3]

Be united, O kings of the earth, for thereby will the tempest of discord be stilled amongst you, and your peoples find rest, if ye be of them that comprehend. Should any one among you take up arms against another, rise ye all against him, for this is naught but manifest justice. *Bahá'u'lláh*[4]

The structure of world stability and order hath been reared upon, and will continue to be sustained by, the twin pillars of reward and punishment. *Bahá'u'lláh*[5]

Justice hath a mighty force at its command. It is none other than reward and punishment for the deeds of men. By the power of this force the tabernacle of order is established throughout the world, causing the wicked to restrain their natures for fear of punishment.

Bahá'u'lláh[6]

If the learned and worldly-wise men of this age were to allow mankind to inhale the fragrance of fellowship and love, every understanding heart would apprehend the meaning of true liberty, and discover the secret of undisturbed peace and absolute composure.

Bahá'u'lláh[7]

Take heed, O concourse of the rulers of the world! There is no force on earth that can equal in its conquering power the force of justice and wisdom . . . Blessed is the king who marcheth with the ensign of wisdom unfurled before him, and the battalions of justice massed in his rear. He verily is the ornament that adorneth the brow of peace and the countenance of security.

Bahá'u'lláh[8]

Verily I say: The fear of God hath ever been a sure defence and a safe stronghold for all the peoples of the world. It is the chief cause of the protection of mankind, and the supreme instrument for its preservation.

Bahá'u'lláh[9]

The Great Being, wishing to reveal the prerequisites of the peace and tranquillity of the world and the advancement of its peoples, hath written: The time must come when the imperative necessity for the holding of a vast, an all-embracing assemblage of men will be universally realized. The rulers and kings of the earth must needs attend it, and, participating in its deliberations, must consider such ways and means as will lay the foundations of the world's Great Peace amongst men. Such a peace demandeth that the Great Powers should resolve, for the sake of the tranquillity of the peoples of the earth, to be fully reconciled among themselves. Should any king take up arms against another, all should unitedly arise and prevent him. If this be done, the nations of the world will no longer require any armaments, except for the purpose of preserving the security of their realms and of maintaining internal order within their territories. This will ensure the peace and composure of every people, government and nation.

Bahá'u'lláh[10]

Governments should fully acquaint themselves with the conditions of those they govern, and confer upon them positions according to desert and merit. It is enjoined upon every ruler and sovereign to consider this matter with the utmost care that the traitor may not usurp the position of the faithful, nor the despoiler rule in the place of the trustworthy. *Bahá'u'lláh*[11]

When the Daystar of Wisdom rose above the horizon of God's Holy Dispensation it voiced this all-glorious utterance: They that are possessed of wealth and invested with authority and power must show the profoundest regard for religion. In truth, religion is a radiant light and an impregnable stronghold for the protection and welfare of the peoples of the world, for the fear of God impelleth man to hold fast to that which is good, and shun all evil. Should the lamp of religion be obscured, chaos and confusion will ensue, and the lights of fairness and justice, of tranquillity and peace cease to shine. Unto this will bear witness every man of true understanding. *Bahá'u'lláh*[12]

We have enjoined upon all mankind to establish the Most Great Peace – the surest of all means for the protection of humanity. The sovereigns of the world should, with one accord, hold fast thereunto, for this is the supreme instrument that can ensure the security and welfare of all peoples and nations. *Bahá'u'lláh*[13]

It is incumbent upon everyone to observe God's holy commandments, inasmuch as they are the wellspring of life unto the world. The heaven of divine wisdom is illumined with the two luminaries of consultation and compassion and the canopy of world order is upraised upon the two pillars of reward and punishment.

Bahá'u'lláh[14]

O concourse of rulers! Give ear unto that which hath been raised from the Dayspring of Grandeur: 'Verily, there is none other God but Me, the Lord of Utterance, the All-Knowing.' Bind ye the broken with the hands of justice, and crush the oppressor who flourisheth with the rod of the commandments of your Lord, the Ordainer, the All-Wise. *Bahá'u'lláh*[15]

Liberty must, in the end, lead to sedition, whose flames none can quench. Thus warneth you He Who is the Reckoner, the All-Knowing. Know ye that the embodiment of liberty and its symbol is the animal. That which beseemeth man is submission unto such restraints as will protect him from his own ignorance, and guard him against the harm of the mischief-maker. Liberty causeth man to overstep the bounds of propriety, and to infringe on the dignity of his station. It debaseth him to the level of extreme depravity and wickedness.

Bahá'u'lláh[16]

Say: True liberty consisteth in man's submission unto My commandments, little as ye know it. Were men to observe that which We have sent down unto them from the Heaven of Revelation, they would, of a certainty, attain unto perfect liberty. *Bahá'u'lláh*[17]

We have decreed that war shall be waged in the path of God with the armies of wisdom and utterance, and of a goodly character and praiseworthy deeds.

Bahá'u'lláh[18]

Beware lest ye shed the blood of any one.

Bahá'u'lláh[19]

In the Book of God, the Mighty, the Great, ye have been forbidden to engage in contention and conflict. Lay fast hold on whatever will profit you, and profit the peoples of the world. *Bahá'u'lláh*[20]

We have abolished the law to wage holy war against each other. *Bahá'u'lláh*[21]

O people! Spread not disorder in the land, and shed not the blood of any one, and consume not the substance of others wrongfully, neither follow every accursed prattler. *Bahá'u'lláh*[22]

It is incumbent upon every man, in this Day, to hold fast unto whatsoever will promote the interests, and exalt the station, of all nations and just governments.

Bahá'u'lláh[23]

We pray God – exalted be His glory – and cherish the hope that He may graciously assist the manifestations of affluence and power and the daysprings of sovereignty and glory, the kings of the earth – may God aid them through His strengthening grace – to establish the Lesser Peace. This, indeed, is the greatest means for insuring the tranquillity of the nations. It is incumbent upon the Sovereigns of the world – may God assist them – unitedly to hold fast unto this Peace, which is the chief instrument for the protection of all mankind. It is Our hope that they will arise to achieve what will be conducive to the well-being of man. It is their duty to convene an all-inclusive assembly, which either they themselves or their ministers will attend, and to enforce whatever measures are required to establish unity and concord amongst men. They must put away the weapons of war, and turn to the instruments of universal reconstruction. Should one king rise up against another, all the other kings must arise to deter him. Arms and armaments will, then, be no more needed beyond that which is necessary to insure the internal security of their respective countries. *Bahá'u'lláh*[24]

O Son of Being! My love is My stronghold; he that entereth therein is safe and secure, and he that turneth away shall surely stray and perish. *Bahá'u'lláh*[25]

The Great Being saith: The heaven of statesmanship is made luminous and resplendent by the brightness of the light of these blessed words which hath dawned from the dayspring of the Will of God: It behoveth every ruler to weigh his own being every day in the balance of equity and justice and then to judge between men and counsel them to do that which would direct their steps unto the path of wisdom and understanding. This is the cornerstone of statesmanship and the essence thereof. From these words every enlightened man of wisdom will readily perceive that which will foster such aims as the welfare, security and protection of mankind and the safety of human lives. *Bahá'u'lláh*[26]

I charge you all that each one of you concentrate all the thoughts of your heart on love and unity. When a thought of war comes, oppose it by a stronger thought of peace. A thought of hatred must be destroyed by a more powerful thought of love. Thoughts of war bring destruction to all harmony, well-being, restfulness and content.

Thoughts of love are constructive of brotherhood, peace, friendship, and happiness.

'Abdu'l-Bahá[27]

13

Selflessness and Service

Happy is the faithful one who is attired with the vesture of high endeavour and hath arisen to serve this Cause. Such a soul hath truly attained the desired Goal and hath apprehended the Object for which it hath been created. *Bahá'u'lláh*[1]

Dedicate thyself to the service of the Cause of thy Lord, cherish His remembrance in thy heart and celebrate His praise in such wise that every wayward and heedless soul may thereby be roused from slumber. *Bahá'u'lláh*[2]

O ye servants of the Merciful One! Arise to serve the Cause of God, in such wise that the cares and sorrows caused by them that have disbelieved in the Dayspring of the Signs of God may not afflict you. At the time when the Promise was fulfilled and the Promised One made manifest, differences have appeared amongst the kindreds of the earth and each people hath followed its own fancy and idle imaginings. *Bahá'u'lláh*[3]

Be not dismayed, O peoples of the world, when the day-star of My beauty is set, and the heaven of My tabernacle is concealed from your eyes. Arise to further My Cause, and to exalt My Word amongst men. We are with you at all times, and shall strengthen you through the power of truth. We are truly almighty. Whoso hath recognized Me will arise and serve Me with such determination that the powers of earth and heaven shall be unable to defeat his purpose. *Bahá'u'lláh*[4]

Make thou every effort to render service unto God, that from thee may appear that which will immortalize thy memory in His glorious and exalted heaven.

Bahá'u'lláh[5]

Beware lest ye commit that which would sadden the hearts of your fathers and mothers. Follow ye the path of Truth which indeed is a straight path. Should anyone give you a choice between the opportunity to render a service to Me and a service to them, choose ye to serve them, and let such service be a path leading you to Me. This is My exhortation and command unto thee. Observe therefore that which thy Lord, the Mighty, the Gracious, hath prescribed unto thee. *Bahá'u'lláh*[6]

O My Servant! Free thyself from the fetters of this world, and loose thy soul from the prison of self. Seize thy chance, for it will come to thee no more.

Bahá'u'lláh[7]

Say: Glorified art Thou, O my God! I implore Thee by the Dawning-Place of Thy signs and by the Revealer of Thy clear tokens to grant that I may, under all conditions, hold fast the cord of Thy loving providence and cling tenaciously to the hem of Thy generosity. Reckon me then with those whom the changes and chances of the world have failed to deter from serving Thee and from bearing allegiance unto Thee, whom the onslaught of the people hath been powerless to hinder from magnifying Thy Name and celebrating Thy praise. Graciously assist me, O my Lord, to do whatever Thou lovest and desirest. Enable me then to fulfil that which will exalt Thy Name and will set ablaze the fire of Thy love.

Thou art, in truth, the Forgiving, the Bountiful.

Bahá'u'lláh[8]

Faith is the magnet which draws the confirmation of the Merciful One. Service is the magnet which attracts the heavenly strength. I hope thou wilt attain both.

'Abdu'l-Bahá[9]

As to the fact that man must entirely forget himself, by this is meant that he should arise in the mystery of sacrifice and that is the disappearance of mortal sentiments and extinction of blamable morals which constitute the temporal gloom, and not that the physical health should be changed into weakness and debility.

'Abdu'l-Bahá[10]

Be ye a refuge to the fearful; bring ye rest and peace to the disturbed; make ye a provision for the destitute; be a treasury of riches for the poor; be a healing medicine for those who suffer pain; be ye doctor and nurse to the ailing; promote ye friendship, and honour, and conciliation, and devotion to God, in this world of non-existence.

'Abdu'l-Bahá[11]

Know that nothing will benefit thee in this life save supplication and invocation unto God, service in His vineyard, and, with a heart full of love, be in constant servitude unto Him. *'Abdu'l-Bahá*[12]

Wherefore, O ye illumined youth, strive by night and by day to unravel the mysteries of the mind and spirit, and to grasp the secrets of the Day of God. Inform yourselves of the evidences that the Most Great Name hath dawned. Open your lips in praise. Adduce convincing arguments and proofs. Lead those who thirst to the fountain of life; grant ye true health to the ailing. Be ye apprentices of God; be ye physicians directed by God, and heal ye the sick among humankind. Bring those who have been excluded into the circle of intimate friends. Make the despairing to be filled with hope. Waken them that slumber; make the heedless mindful.

Such are the fruits of this earthly life. Such is the station of resplendent glory. Upon you be Bahá'u'l-Abhá. *'Abdu'l-Bahá*[13]

14

The Need for Personal Transformation

O My Friends! Have ye forgotten that true and radiant morn, when in those hallowed and blessed surroundings ye were all gathered in My presence beneath the shade of the tree of life, which is planted in the all-glorious paradise? Awe-struck ye listened as I gave utterance to these three most holy words: O friends! Prefer not your will to Mine, never desire that which I have not desired for you, and approach Me not with lifeless hearts, defiled with worldly desires and cravings. Would ye but sanctify your souls, ye would at this present hour recall that place and those surroundings, and the truth of My utterance should be made evident unto all of you.

Bahá'u'lláh[1]

O Son of Spirit! My first counsel is this: Possess a pure, kindly and radiant heart, that thine may be a sovereignty ancient, imperishable and everlasting.

Bahá'u'lláh[2]

Create in me a pure heart, O my God, and renew a tranquil conscience within me, O my Hope! Through the spirit of power confirm Thou me in Thy Cause, O my Best-Beloved, and by the light of Thy glory reveal unto me Thy path, O Thou the Goal of my desire! Through the power of Thy transcendent might lift me up unto the heaven of Thy holiness, O Source of my being, and by the breezes of Thine eternity gladden me, O Thou Who art my God! Let Thine everlasting melodies breathe tranquillity on me, O my Companion, and let the riches of Thine ancient countenance deliver me from all except Thee, O my Master, and let the tidings of the revelation of Thine incorruptible Essence bring me joy, O Thou Who art the most manifest of the manifest and the most hidden of the hidden! *Bahá'u'lláh*[3]

O Son of Man! Rejoice in the gladness of thine heart, that thou mayest be worthy to meet Me and to mirror forth My beauty. *Bahá'u'lláh*[4]

Become as true brethren in the one and indivisible religion of God, free from distinction, for verily God desireth that your hearts should become mirrors unto your brethren in the Faith, so that ye find yourselves reflected in them, and they in you. This is the true Path of God, the Almighty, and He is indeed watchful over your actions. *The Báb*[5]

It is seemly that the servant should, after each prayer, supplicate God to bestow mercy and forgiveness upon his parents. Thereupon God's call will be raised: 'Thousand upon thousand of what thou hast asked for thy parents shall be thy recompense!' Blessed is he who remembereth his parents when communing with God.

There is, verily, no God but Him, the Mighty, the Well-Beloved. *The Báb*[6]

Withhold thy tongue from uttering that which might grieve thee and beseech God for mercy. Verily He is fully cognizant of the righteous, for He is with such of His servants as truly believe in Him, and He is not unaware of the actions of the mischief-makers, inasmuch as nothing whatever in the heavens or on the earth can escape His knowledge. *The Báb*[7]

Between material things and spiritual things there is a connection. The more healthful his body the greater will be the power of the spirit of man; the power of the intellect, the power of the memory, the power of reflection will then be greater. *'Abdu'l-Bahá*[8]

I hope thou wilt become as a rising light and obtain spiritual health – and spiritual health is conducive to physical health . . . *'Abdu'l-Bahá*[9]

And if thou art looking for the divine remedy which will cure the spirit of man of all diseases and make him obtain the health of the divine Kingdom, know that it is the precepts and teaching of God. Take the greatest care of them. *'Abdu'l-Bahá*[10]

You must live in the utmost happiness. If any trouble or vicissitude comes into your lives, if your heart is depressed on account of health, livelihood or vocation, let not these things affect you. They should not cause unhappiness, for Bahá'u'lláh has brought you divine happiness. He has prepared heavenly food for you; He has destined eternal bounty for you . . . *'Abdu'l-Bahá*[11]

Truthfulness is the foundation of all human virtues. Without truthfulness progress and success, in all the worlds of God, are impossible for any soul. When this holy attribute is established in man, all the divine qualities will also be acquired. *'Abdu'l-Bahá*[12]

Prayer

Thou knowest full well, O my God, that tribulations have showered upon me from all directions and that no one can dispel or transmute them except Thee. I know of a certainty, by virtue of my love for Thee, that Thou wilt never cause tribulations to befall any soul unless Thou desirest to exalt his station in Thy celestial Paradise and to buttress his heart in this earthly life with the bulwark of Thine all-compelling power, that it may not become inclined toward the vanities of this world. Indeed Thou art well aware that under all conditions I would cherish the remembrance of Thee far more than the ownership of all that is in the heavens and on the earth.

Strengthen my heart, O my God, in Thine obedience and in Thy love and grant that I may be clear of the entire company of Thine adversaries. Verily I swear by Thy glory that I yearn for naught besides Thyself, nor do I desire anything except Thy mercy, nor am I apprehensive of aught save Thy justice. I beg Thee to forgive me as well as those whom Thou lovest, howsoever Thou pleasest. Verily Thou art the Almighty, the Bountiful.

Immensely exalted art Thou, O Lord of the heavens and earth, above the praise of all men, and may peace be upon Thy faithful servants and glory be unto God, the Lord of all the worlds. *The Báb*[13]

Hidden Dragons

There are dangers on the path to personal transformation. Substances, attitudes, life styles and so on that may appear to be harmless on the surface but which can be blockages to our spiritual growth and development.

From time to time we may find ourselves tested and even tempted. 'One drink won't hurt,' our friends say; or, 'A little of this will help you attain real spiritual awareness,' they insist. 'This is a viable alternative life style,' another may assert.

Let us explore together what the writings of Bahá'u-'lláh, 'Abdu'l-Bahá, Shoghi Effendi and the Universal House of Justice have to say about some of these 'hidden dragons'.

> Yield not to grief and sorrow: they cause the greatest misery. Jealousy consumeth the body and anger doth burn the liver: avoid these two as you would a lion.
> *Bahá'u'lláh*[14]

> O My Servant! Purge thy heart from malice and, innocent of envy, enter the divine court of holiness.
> *Bahá'u'lláh*[15]

> My meaning is that in the sight of God, smoking tobacco is deprecated, abhorrent, filthy in the extreme; and, albeit by degrees, highly injurious to

health. It is also a waste of money and time, and maketh the user a prey to a noxious addiction.

'Abdu'l-Bahá[16]

Regarding the use of liquor: According to the text of the Book of Aqdas, both light and strong drinks are prohibited. The reason for this prohibition is that alcohol leadeth the mind astray and causeth the weakening of the body. *'Abdu'l-Bahá*[17]

Alcohol consumeth the mind and causeth man to commit acts of absurdity . . . *'Abdu'l-Bahá*[18]

. . . Bahá'ís should not use hallucinogenic agents, including LSD, peyote and similar substances, except when prescribed for medical treatment. Neither should they become involved in experiments with such substances.

Although we have found no direct reference to marijuana in the Bahá'í writings, since this substance is derived from what is considered to be a milder form of cannabis, the species used to produce hashish, we can share with you a translation from the Persian of a Tablet of 'Abdu'l-Bahá on hashish:

'Regarding hashish you had pointed out that some Persians have become habituated to its use. Gracious God! This is the worst of all intoxicants, and its prohibition is explicitly revealed. Its use causeth the disintegration of thought and the complete torpor of the soul. How could anyone seek this fruit of the infernal tree, and by partaking of it, be led to exemplify the qualities of a monster? How could one use this forbidden drug, and thus deprive himself of the blessings of the All-Merciful?'

The Universal House of Justice[19]

Concerning the so-called 'spiritual' virtues of the hallucinogens . . . spiritual stimulation should come from turning one's heart to Bahá'u'lláh, and not through physical means such as drugs and agents.

From the description given in your letter it appears that hallucinogenic agents are a form of intoxicant. As the friends, including the youth, are required strictly to abstain from all forms of intoxicants, and are further expected conscientiously to obey the civil law of their country, it is obvious that they should refrain from using these drugs.

A very great responsibility for the future peace and well-being of the world is borne by the youth of today. Let the Bahá'í youth by the power of the Cause they espouse be the shining example for their companions.

The Universal House of Justice[20]

. . . a chaste and holy life . . . calls for the abandonment of a frivolous conduct, with its excessive attachment to trivial and often misdirected pleasures. It requires total abstinence from all alcoholic drinks, from opium, and from similar habit-forming drugs. It condemns the prostitution of art and of literature, the practices of nudism and of companionate marriage, infidelity in marital relationships, and all manner of promiscuity, of easy familiarity, and of sexual vices. It can tolerate no compromise with the theories, the standards, the habits, and the excesses of a decadent age. Nay rather it seeks to demonstrate, through the dynamic force of its example, the pernicious character of such theories, the falsity of such standards, the hollowness of such claims, the perversity of such habits, and the sacrilegious character of such excesses.

Shoghi Effendi[21]

The Bahá'í Faith recognizes the value of the sex impulse, but condemns its illegitimate and improper expression such as free love, companionate marriage and others, all of which it considers positively harmful to man and to the society in which he lives. The proper use of the sex instinct is the natural right of every individual, and it is precisely for this very purpose that the institution of marriage has been established. The Bahá'ís do not believe in the suppression of the sex impulse but in its regulation and control.

Written on behalf of Shoghi Effendi[22]

Homosexuality, according to the Writings of Bahá'u-'lláh, is spiritually condemned. This does not mean that people so afflicted must not be helped and advised and sympathized with. It does mean that we do not believe that it is a permissible way of life . . .

Written on behalf of Shoghi Effendi[23]

15

Prayer and Contemplation

Preparation for Prayer

When you wish to pray, it is important first to perform your ablutions and then go into a private place where you can be alone for a while. Take some time to quiet the mind and centre your thoughts on the Beloved. If you wish to offer Him a gift, anoint yourself with a little rose water. If you find it difficult to centre your mind, closing your eyes and listening to some gently spiritual music may be helpful before you being your prayers.

Ablutions

> It hath been ordained that every believer in God, the Lord of Judgement, shall, each day, having washed his hands and then his face, seat himself and, turning unto God, repeat 'Alláh-u-Abhá' ninety-five times. Such was the decree of the Maker of the Heavens when, with majesty and power, He established Himself upon the thrones of His Names. Perform ye, likewise, ablutions for the Obligatory Prayer; this is the command of God, the Incomparable, the Unrestrained.
>
> *Bahá'u'lláh*[1]

Simple prayer beads to help you in the recitation of 'Alláh-u-Abhá' may be made by stringing 95 wooden or stone beads onto a strong cord or thong and forming a secure knot at the end.

> Make use of rose-water, and of pure perfume; this, indeed, is that which God hath loved from the beginning that hath no beginning, in order that there may be diffused from you what your Lord, the Incomparable, the All-Wise, desireth. *Bahá'u'lláh*[2]

Rosewater, attar of rose and pure perfume (essential oils) are all made from the natural plant substance. Avoid chemical imitations (for example, most commercial perfumes), as they will not have the same effect. Rosewater, attar of rose and essential oils are obtainable at some health food stores or through a supplier of aromatherapy products.

> God loveth those who are pure. Naught in the Bayán and in the sight of God is more loved than purity and immaculate cleanliness . . . *The Báb*[3]

Privacy

> The reason why privacy hath been enjoined in moments of devotion is this, that thou mayest give thy best attention to the remembrance of God, that thy heart may at all times be animated with His Spirit, and not be shut out as by a veil from thy Best Beloved. Let not thy tongue pay lip service in praise of God while thy heart be not attuned to the exalted Summit of Glory, and the Focal Point of communion.
>
> *The Báb*[4]

Silence

It behoveth you to remain silent before His Throne, for indeed of all the things which have been created between heaven and earth nothing on that Day will be deemed more fitting than the observance of silence.
The Báb[5]

Detachment

O Son of Light! Forget all save Me and commune with My spirit. This is of the essence of My command, therefore turn unto it. *Bahá'u'lláh*[6]

Rid thou thyself of all attachments to aught except God, enrich thyself in God by dispensing with all else besides Him, and recite this prayer:

> Say: God sufficeth all things above all things, and nothing in the heavens or in the earth or in whatever lieth between them but God, thy Lord, sufficeth. Verily, He is in Himself the Knower, the Sustainer, the Omnipotent.
> *The Báb*[7]

The most acceptable prayer is the one offered with the utmost spirituality and radiance; its prolongation hath not been and is not beloved by God. The more detached and the purer the prayer, the more acceptable is it in the presence of God. *The Báb*[8]

Direction of Prayer

Facing in the direction of the Qiblih is a fixed requirement for the recitation of obligatory prayer, but for other prayers and devotions one may follow what the merciful Lord hath revealed in the Qur'án: 'Whichever way ye turn, there is the face of God.' *Bahá'u'lláh*[9]

If we wish to pray we must have some object upon which to concentrate. If we turn to God we must direct our hearts to a certain centre. If man worships God otherwise than through his Manifestation he must first form a conception of God and that conception is created by his own mind. As the finite cannot comprehend the Infinite so God is not to be comprehended in this fashion. That which he can comprehend is not God. That conception of God which a man has is but a phantasm, an image, an imagination, an illusion. There is no connection between such a conception and the Supreme Being. *Attributed to 'Abdu'l-Bahá*[10]

Contemplation, Meditation

O people of the earth! Appreciate the value of this heavenly word. Indeed it may be likened unto a ship for the ocean of knowledge and a shining luminary for the realm of perception. *Bahá'u'lláh*[11]

Our spiritual perception, our inward sight must be opened, so that we can see the signs and traces of God's spirit in everything. Everything can reflect to us the light of the Spirit. *'Abdu'l-Bahá*[12]

Meditation is the key for opening the doors of mysteries. In that state man abstracts himself: in that state man withdraws himself from all outside objects; in that subjective mood he is immersed in the ocean of spiritual life and can unfold the secrets of things-in-themselves. To illustrate this, think of man as endowed with two kinds of sight; when the power of insight is being used the outward power of vision does not see.

This faculty of meditation frees man from the animal nature, discerns the reality of things, puts man in touch with God.

This faculty brings forth from the invisible plane the sciences and arts. Through the meditative faculty inventions are made possible, colossal undertakings are carried out; through it governments can run smoothly.

Through this faculty man enters into the very Kingdom of God. *'Abdu'l-Bahá*[13]

But if He appeareth while thou hast turned unto thyself in meditation, this shall not profit thee, unless thou shalt mention His Name by words He hath revealed. *The Báb*[14]

Praise

Through the radiance of His light God imparteth illumination to your hearts and maketh firm your steps, that perchance ye may yield praise unto Him. *The Báb*[15]

Communion

Man is eternally in a state of communion and prayer with the source of all good. The highest and most elevating state is the state of prayer. Prayer is communion with God . . . Its efficacy is conditional upon the freedom of the heart from extraneous suggestions and mundane thoughts. The worshipper must pray with a detached spirit, unconditional surrender of the will, concentrated attention and a magnetic spiritual passion. His innermost being must be stirred with the ethereal breeze of holiness. If the mirror of his life is polished from the dross of all desires the heavenly pictures and star-like images of the kingdom of God will become fully reflected therein. Then he will be given power to translate these celestial forms into his own daily life and the lives of many thousands.

Attributed to 'Abdu'l-Bahá[16]

Draw nigh unto God and persevere in (thy) communion with (or prayer to) thy Lord, so that the fire of God's love may glow more luminously in the heart, its heat grow stronger and give warmth to that region and its sound reach the Supreme Concourse.

'Abdu'l-Bahá[17]

Conversation

The wisdom of prayer is this: That it causeth a connection between the servant and the True One, because in that state man with all heart and soul turneth his face towards His Highness the Almighty, seeking His association and desiring His love and compassion. The greatest happiness for a lover is to converse with his beloved, and the greatest gift for a seeker is to become familiar with the object of his longing; that is why with every soul who is attracted to the Kingdom of God, his greatest hope is to find an opportunity to entreat and supplicate before his Beloved, appeal for His mercy and grace and be immersed in the ocean of His utterance, goodness and generosity. *'Abdu'l-Bahá*[18]

There is nothing sweeter in the world of existence than prayer.

Man must live in a state of prayer. The most blessed condition is the condition of prayer and supplication. Prayer is conversation with God. The greatest attainment or the sweetest state is none other than conversation with God. It creates spirituality, creates mindfulness and celestial feelings, begets new attractions of the Kingdom and engenders the susceptibilities of the higher intelligence. The highest attribute given to his holiness Moses is the following verse: 'God carried along a conversation with Moses.'

Attributed to 'Abdu'l-Bahá[19]

The Prayerful Attitude

The prayerful attitude is attained by two means. Just as a man who is going to deliver a lecture prepares therefor and his preparation consists of certain meditations and notations, so the preparation for the prayerful attitude is detaching one's mind from all other thoughts save the thought of God at the time of prayer and then praying when the prayful attitude shall be attained. *Attributed to 'Abdu'l-Bahá*[20]

Prayer and supplication are two wings whereby man soars toward the heavenly mansion of the True One. However, verbal repetition of prayer does not suffice, One must live in a continual attitude of prayer. When man is spiritually free his mind becomes the altar of prayer and his heart the sanctuary of prayer. Then the meaning of the verse, 'We will lift up from before his eyes the veil', will become fulfilled in him.

'Abdu'l-Bahá[21]

Supplication

In response to the question 'Why pray?' 'Abdu'l-Bahá answered:

Know thou, verily, it is becoming in a weak one to supplicate to the Strong One, and it behoveth a seeker of bounty to beseech the Glorious Bountiful One.

When one supplicates to his Lord, turns to Him and seeks bounty from His Ocean, this supplication brings light to his heart, illumination to his sight, life to his soul and exaltation to his being. *'Abdu'l-Bahá*[22]

Turn thy face sincerely toward God; be severed from all save God; be ablaze with the fire of the love of God; be purified and sanctified, and beseech and supplicate God. Verily, he responds unto those who invoke him, is near unto those who pray unto him. And he is thy companion in every loneliness, and befriends every exile. *'Abdu'l-Bahá*[23]

Supplication to God at morn and eve is conducive to the joy of hearts, and prayer causes spirituality and fragrance. Thou shouldst necessarily continue therein. *'Abdu'l-Bahá*[24]

Mysteries of God

Thou hast written what shouldst thou do and what prayer shouldst thou offer in order to become informed of the mysteries of God: Pray thou with an attracted heart and supplicate with a spirit stirred by the glad tidings of God. Then the doors of the kingdom of mysteries shall be opened before thy face, and thou shalt comprehend the realities of all things. *'Abdu'l-Bahá*[25]

Love of God

If one friend feels love for another he will wish to say so. Though he knows that the friend is aware that he loves him, he will still wish to say so. If there is anyone that you love do you not seek an opportunity to speak with him, to speak lovingly with him, to bring him gifts, to write him letters? If you do not feel such a desire it would be that you did not love your friend. God knows the wishes of all hearts. But the impulse to pray is a natural one springing from man's love to God. *'Abdu'l-Bahá*[26]

Creating an Environment for Prayer and Contemplation

You may wish to set aside a special space just for prayer and contemplation. This place can be as simple or elaborate as your resources and imagination allow.

My first prayer space consisted of some orange crates, a large scarf, a framed picture of Jesus (we were Episcopalians) and a candle. So simple, yet I still remember the wondrous feeling of being in that special place.

A comfortable chair or place to sit and a light source are the only absolute requirements. You may wish to consider adding a small bookcase – one about the height of your arms as you sit in your chair would be helpful, as you could use the top shelf for items such as your prayer book, rose water, prayer beads, picture of the Shrine of Bahá'u'lláh, candle holder and so on. Everything you place there should be meaningful and precious to you.

The lower shelves could accommodate the books and music you choose to have near you during your quiet times.

How delightful it is to have a place of your very own, where you can feel warmly comfortable and deeply at home. A place where you can commune with your

Beloved and learn more about Him every day. A refuge you can come to when in need of rest or healing and know you will find comfort and peace therein.

16

Social and Economic Development

All men have been created to carry forward an ever-advancing civilization. *Bahá'u'lláh*[1]

These are not days of prosperity and triumph. The whole of mankind is in the grip of manifold ills. Strive, therefore, to save its life through the wholesome medicine which the almighty hand of the unerring Physician hath prepared. *Bahá'u'lláh*[2]

The progress of the world, the development of nations, the tranquillity of peoples, and the peace of all who dwell on earth are among the principles and ordinances of God. Religion bestoweth upon man the most precious of all gifts, offereth the cup of prosperity, imparteth eternal life, and showereth imperishable benefits upon mankind. *Bahá'u'lláh*[3]

. . . in order to establish a better social order and economic condition, there must be allegiance to the laws and principles of government. *'Abdu'l-Bahá*[4]

The development and progress of a nation is according to the measure and degree of that nation's scientific attainments. Through this means its greatness is continually increased, and day by day the welfare and prosperity of its people are assured. *'Abdu'l-Bahá*[5]

. . . is there any deed in the world that would be nobler than service to the common good? Is there any greater blessing conceivable for a man, than that he should become the cause of the education, the development, the prosperity and honour of his fellow-creatures? No, by the Lord God! The highest righteousness of all is for blessed souls to take hold of the hands of the helpless and deliver them out of their ignorance and abasement and poverty, and with pure motives, and only for the sake of God, to arise and energetically devote themselves to the service of the masses, forgetting their own worldly advantage and working only to serve the general good. *'Abdu'l-Bahá*[6]

The unity of the human race, as envisaged by Bahá'u'lláh, implies the establishment of a world commonwealth in which all nations, races, creeds and classes are closely and permanently united . . . The economic resources of the world will be organized, its sources of raw materials will be tapped and fully utilized, its markets will be coordinated and developed, and the distribution of its products will be equitably regulated . . . Destitution on the one hand, and gross accumulation of ownership on the other, will disappear.

Shoghi Effendi[7]

We have enjoined upon all to become engaged in some trade or profession, and have accounted such occupation to be an act of worship. Before all else, however, thou shouldst receive, as a sign of God's acceptance, the mantle of trustworthiness from the hands of divine favour; for trustworthiness is the chief means of attracting confirmation and prosperity. We entreat God to make of it a radiant and mercifully showering rain-cloud that shall bring success and blessings to thy affairs. He of a truth is the All-Bountiful, the Gracious.

Bahá'u'lláh[8]

Commerce, agriculture and industry should not, in truth, be a bar to service of the one true God. Indeed, such occupations are most potent instruments and clear proofs for the manifestation of the evidences of one's piety, of one's trustworthiness and of the virtues of the All-Merciful Lord. *'Abdu'l-Bahá*[9]

The learned of the day must direct the people to acquire those branches of knowledge which are of use, that both the learned themselves and the generality of mankind may derive benefits therefrom. Such academic pursuits as begin and end in words alone have never been and will never be of any worth. *Bahá'u'lláh*[10]

Economy is the foundation of human prosperity. The spendthrift is always in trouble. Prodigality on the part of any person is an unpardonable sin. We must never live on others like a parasitic plant . . . It is more kingly to be satisfied with a crust of stale bread than to enjoy a sumptuous dinner of many courses, the money for which comes out of the pockets of others.

'Abdu'l-Bahá[11]

The rich, but for a few, shall in no wise attain the court of His presence nor enter the city of content and resignation. *Bahá'u'lláh*[12]

Please God, the poor may exert themselves and strive to earn the means of livelihood. This is a duty which, in this most great Revelation, hath been prescribed unto every one, and is accounted in the sight of God as a goodly deed. Whoso observeth this duty, the help of the invisible One shall most certainly aid him.

Bahá'u'lláh[13]

Waste not your time in idleness and sloth. Occupy yourselves with that which profiteth yourselves and others. *Bahá'u'lláh*[14]

How sad if any man were, in this Day, to rest his heart on the transitory things of this world! *Bahá'u'lláh*[15]

The world is but a show, vain and empty, a mere nothing, bearing the semblance of reality. Set not your affections upon it. *Bahá'u'lláh*[16]

The civilization, so often vaunted by the learned exponents of arts and sciences, will, if allowed to overleap the bounds of moderation, bring great evil upon men. Thus warneth you He Who is the All-Knowing. If carried to excess, civilization will prove as prolific a source of evil as it had been of goodness when kept within the restraints of moderation. *Bahá'u'lláh*[17]

O friends! Help ye the one true God, exalted be His glory, by your goodly deeds, by such conduct and character as shall be acceptable in His sight. He that seeketh to be a helper of God in this Day, let him close his eyes to whatever he may possess, and open them to the things of God. *Bahá'u'lláh*[18]

17

Justice and Human Rights

O Son of Spirit! The best beloved of all things in My sight is Justice; turn not away therefrom if thou desirest Me, and neglect it not that I may confide in thee. By its aid thou shalt see with thine own eyes and not through the eyes of others, and shalt know of thine own knowledge and not through the knowledge of thy neighbour. Ponder this in thy heart; how it behoveth thee to be. Verily justice is My gift to thee and the sign of My loving-kindness. Set it then before thine eyes.

Bahá'u'lláh[1]

O people of God! That which traineth the world is Justice, for it is upheld by two pillars, reward and punishment. These two pillars are the sources of life to the world.

Bahá'u'lláh[2]

The light of men is Justice. Quench it not with the contrary winds of oppression and tyranny. The purpose of justice is the appearance of unity among men.

Bahá'u'lláh[3]

We ask God to endow human souls with justice so that they may be fair, and may strive to provide for the comfort of all, that each member of humanity may pass his life in the utmost comfort and welfare. Then this material world will become the very paradise of the Kingdom, this elemental earth will be in a heavenly state and all the servants of God will live in the utmost joy, happiness and gladness. We must all strive and concentrate all our thoughts in order that such happiness may accrue to the world of humanity.

'Abdu'l-Bahá[4]

The primary purpose, the basic objective, in laying down powerful laws and setting up great principles and institutions dealing with every aspect of civilization, is human happiness; and human happiness consists only in drawing closer to the Threshold of Almighty God, and in securing the peace and well-being of every individual member, high and low alike, of the human race; and the supreme agencies for accomplishing these two objectives are the excellent qualities with which humanity has been endowed. *'Abdu'l-Bahá*[5]

They that are just and fair-minded in their judgement occupy a sublime station and hold an exalted rank. The light of piety and uprightness shineth resplendent from these souls. We earnestly hope that the peoples and countries of the world may not be deprived of the splendours of these two luminaries. *Bahá'u'lláh*[6]

O kings of Christendom! . . . God hath committed into your hands the reins of the government of the people, that ye may rule with justice over them, safeguard the rights of the down-trodden, and punish the wrongdoers. If ye neglect the duty prescribed unto you by God in His Book, your names shall be numbered with those of the unjust in His sight. Grievous, indeed, will be your error.

Bahá'u'lláh[7]

We exhort the men of the House of Justice and command them to ensure the protection and safeguarding of men, women and children. It is incumbent upon them to have the utmost regard for the interests of the people at all times and under all conditions. Blessed is the ruler who succoureth the captive, and the rich one who careth for the poor, and the just one who secureth from the wrong doer the rights of the downtrodden, and happy the trustee who observeth that which the Ordainer, the Ancient of Days hath prescribed unto him.

Bahá'u'lláh[8]

We entreat God to deliver the light of equity and the sun of justice from the thick clouds of waywardness, and cause them to shine forth upon men. No light can compare with the light of justice. The establishment of order in the world and the tranquillity of the nations depend upon it.

Bahá'u'lláh[9]

Kings must rule with wisdom and justice; prince, peer and peasant alike have equal rights to just treatment, there must be no favour shown to individuals.

'Abdu'l-Bahá[10]

When perfect justice reigns in every country of the Eastern and Western World, then will the earth become a place of beauty. The dignity and equality of every servant of God will be acknowledged; the ideal of the solidarity of the human race, the true brotherhood of man, will be realized; and the glorious light of the Sun of Truth will illumine the souls of all men.

'Abdu'l-Bahá[11]

Equality and Brotherhood must be established among all members of mankind. This is according to Justice. The general rights of mankind must be guarded and preserved.

All men must be treated equally. This is inherent in the very nature of humanity. *'Abdu'l-Bahá*[12]

Other attributes of perfection are to fear God, to love God by loving His servants, to exercise mildness and forbearance and calm, to be sincere, amenable, clement and compassionate; to have resolution and courage, trustworthiness and energy, to strive and struggle, to be generous, loyal, without malice, to have zeal and a sense of honour, to be high-minded and magnanimous, and to have regard for the rights of others. Whoever is lacking in these excellent human qualities is defective.

'Abdu'l-Bahá[13]

Every human being has the right to live; they have a right to rest, and to a certain amount of well-being. As a rich man is able to live in his palace surrounded by luxury and the greatest comfort, so should a poor man be able to have the necessaries of life. Nobody should die of hunger; everybody should have sufficient clothing; one man should not live in excess while another has no possible means of existence.

Let us try with all the strength we have to bring about happier conditions, so that no single soul may be destitute.

'Abdu'l-Bahá[14]

One of the most important principles of the Teaching of Bahá'u'lláh is:

The right of every human being to the daily bread whereby they exist, or the equalization of the means of livelihood.

The arrangements of the circumstances of the people must be such that poverty shall disappear, that everyone, as far as possible, according to his rank and position, shall share in comfort and well-being.

'Abdu'l-Bahá[15]

Women have equal rights with men upon earth; in religion and society they are a very important element. As long as women are prevented from attaining their highest possibilities, so long will men be unable to achieve the greatness which might be theirs.

'Abdu'l-Bahá[16]

Bibliography

'Abdu'l-Bahá. *Foundations of World Unity*. Wilmette, Ill.: Bahá'í Publishing Trust, 1945.

Paris Talks. London: Bahá'í Publishing Trust, 1961.

— *The Secret of Divine Civilization*. Wilmette, Ill.: Bahá'í Publishing Trust, 1990.

— *Selections from the Writings of 'Abdu'l-Bahá*. Haifa: Bahá'í World Centre, 1978.

— *Tablets of Abdul-Baha Abbas*. New York: Bahá'í Publishing Committee; vol. 1, 1930; vol. 2, 1940; vol. 3, 1930.

'Abdu'l-Bahá in London. London: Bahá'í Publishing Trust, 1987.

Bahá'í World Faith. Wilmette, Ill.: Bahá'í Publishing Trust, 2nd edn. 1976.

Bahá'u'lláh. *Epistle to the Son of the Wolf*. Wilmette, Ill.: Bahá'í Publishing Trust, 1988.

— *Gleanings from the Writings of Bahá'u'lláh*. Wilmette, Ill.: Bahá'í Publishing Trust, 1983.

— *The Hidden Words*. Wilmette, Ill.: Bahá'í Publishing Trust, 1990.

— *The Kitáb-i-Aqdas*. Haifa: Bahá'í World Centre, 1992.

— *Kitáb-i-Íqán*. Wilmette, Ill.: Bahá'í Publishing Trust, 1989.

— *Prayers and Meditations*. Wilmette, Ill.: Bahá'í Publishing Trust, 1987.

— *The Seven Valleys and the Four Valleys*. Wilmette, Ill.: Bahá'í Publishing Trust, 1991.

— *Tablets of Bahá'u'lláh*. Wilmette, Ill.: Bahá'í Publishing Trust, 1988.

Compilation of Compilations, The. Prepared by the Universal House of Justice 1963–1990. 2 vols. [Sydney]: Bahá'í Publications Australia, 1991.

Gail, Marzieh. *Bahá'í Glossary*. Wilmette, Ill.: Bahá'í Publishing Trust, 1957.

Lights of Guidance: A Bahá'í Reference File. Compiled by Helen Hornby. New Delhi: Bahá'í Publishing Trust, 2nd edn. 1988.

Star of the West. Rpt. Oxford: George Ronald, 1984.

References

Preface

1. ‘Abdu’l-Bahá, *Selections*, p. 252.

Chapter 1: ***Keys for Unlocking the Creative Word***

1. Bahá’u’lláh, *Tablets of Bahá’u’lláh*, p. 173.
2. ‘Abdu’l-Bahá, in *Compilation*, vol. 1, p. 292.
3. Bahá’u’lláh, in *Bahá’í World Faith*, p. 204.
4. Gail, *Bahá’í Glossary*, p. 25.
5. Bahá’u’lláh, *Gleanings*, p. 185.
6. ibid. p. 326.
7. ‘Abdu’l-Bahá, *Selections*, pp. 110–11.
8. The Báb, *Selections*, p. 99.
9. ‘Abdu’l-Bahá, in *Compilation*, vol. 2, p. 338.
10. ibid.
11. Bahá’u’lláh, *Tablets*, p. 200.
12. Báb, *Selections*, p. 99.
13. Bahá’u’lláh, *Gleanings*, p. 295.
14. ‘Abdu’l-Bahá, in *Compilation*, vol. 2, p. 76.
15. Bahá’u’lláh, *Gleanings*, p. 201.
16. ibid. p. 289.
17. From a letter written on behalf of Shoghi Effendi, 6 October 1954, in *Compilation*, vol. 1, pp. 231–2.
18. National Teaching Committee of the United States, July 1994, quoting a letter written on behalf of Shoghi Effendi, 11 March 1956, in *Compilation*, vol. 1, p. 232, and ‘Abdu’l-Bahá, in ibid. p. 199.

Chapter 2: ***One God***

1. Bahá'u'lláh, *Epistle to the Son of the Wolf*, p. 1.
2. ibid. p. 13.
3. ibid. p. 37.
4. Bahá'u'lláh, *Prayers and Meditations*, p. 28.
5. Bahá'u'lláh, *Epistle to the Son of the Wolf*, p. 43.
6. ibid. p. 3.
7. Quoted by Bahá'u'lláh in *Seven Valleys*, p. 61.
8. Bahá'u'lláh, *Epistle to the Son of the Wolf*, p. 98.
9. ibid. p. 3.
10. Bahá'u'lláh, *Prayers and Meditations*, pp. 86–7.
11. ibid. p. 33.
12. Bahá'u'lláh, *Tablets*, p. 231.
13. Bahá'u'lláh, *Prayers and Meditation*, pp. 57–8.
14. ibid. pp. 59–60.
15. ibid. p. 80.
16. ibid. pp. 90–1.
17. ibid. pp. 112–13.
18. ibid. p. 115.
19. ibid. p. 117.
20. ibid. p. 119.
21. ibid. p. 250.
22. ibid. p. 274.
23. ibid. p. 130.
24. ibid. p. 172.
25. ibid. p. 222.
26. ibid. p. 282.
27. ibid. p. 334.
28. ibid. p. 295.
29. ibid. pp. 328–9.
30. ibid. p. 324.
31. ibid. p. 329.
32. ibid.
33. ibid. p. 334.
34. Bahá'u'lláh, *Gleanings*, p. 96.
35. Bahá'u'lláh, *Tablets*, pp. 211–12.

36. ibid. p. 114.

Chapter 3: ***Oneness of Humankind***

1. Bahá'u'lláh, *Gleanings*, p. 288.
2. ibid.
3. ibid. p. 289.
4. Bahá'u'lláh, *Epistle to the Son of the Wolf*, p. 2.
5. Bahá'u'lláh, *Gleanings*, p. 250.
6. Bahá'u'lláh, *Kitáb-i-Íqán*, pp. 112–13.
7. Bahá'u'lláh, *Epistle to the Son of the Wolf*, p. 13.
8. ibid. p. 24.
9. ibid. p. 38.
10. ibid. p. 76.
11. Bahá'u'lláh, *Gleanings*, p. 95.
12. ibid. p. 140.
13. ibid. p. 214.
14. Bahá'u'lláh, *Kitáb-i-Íqán*, p. 101.
15. ibid. p. 138.
16. Bahá'u'lláh, *Gleanings*, p. 81.
17. ibid. p. 250.
18. ibid. p. 255.
19. ibid. p. 334.
20. ibid. p. 260.
21. Bahá'u'lláh, *Seven Valleys*, p. 34.
22. Bahá'u'lláh, *Tablets*, p. 129.
23. Bahá'u'lláh, *Epistle to the Son of the Wolf*, p. 26.

Chapter 4: ***Independent Investigation of Truth***

1. Bahá'u'lláh, *Gleanings*, p. 267.
2. Bahá'u'lláh, *Tablets*, p. 249.
3. Bahá'u'lláh, *Gleanings*, p. 268.
4. Bahá'u'lláh, *Kitáb-i-Íqán*, p. 31.
5. Bahá'u'lláh, *Gleanings*, p. 177.
6. ibid. pp. 265–6.
7. ibid. pp. 320–1.

8. ibid. pp. 323–4.
9. Bahá'u'lláh, *Kitáb-i-Íqán*, pp. 3–4.
10. Bahá'u'lláh, *Epistle to the Son of the Wolf*, p. 9.
11. Bahá'u'lláh, *Kitáb-i-Íqán*, p. 47.
12. ibid. pp. 68–9.
13. Bahá'u'lláh, *Epistle to the Son of the Wolf*, p. 115.
14. ibid. p. 150.
15. Bahá'u'lláh, *Tablets*, p. 43.
16. Bahá'u'lláh, *Hidden Words*, Arabic no. 2.

Chapter 5: **The Common Foundation of All Religions**

1. Bahá'u'lláh, *Epistle to the Son of the Wolf*, p. 13.
2. Bahá'u'lláh, *Tablets*, p. 125.
3. Bahá'u'lláh, *Epistle to the Son of the Wolf*, p. 28.
4. Bahá'u'lláh, *Gleanings*, pp. 156–7.
5. Bahá'u'lláh, *Tablets*, p. 168.
6. ibid. p. 22.
7. ibid. p. 129.
8. Bahá'u'lláh, *Kitáb-i-Íqán*, p. 152.
9. ibid. pp. 152–3.
10. ibid. p. 153.
11. ibid.
12. ibid.
13. Bahá'u'lláh, *Kitáb-i-Aqdas*, para. 99.
14. ibid. para. 144.
15. ibid. para. 182.
16. Bahá'u'lláh, *Tablets*, pp. 35–6.

Chapter 6: **The Essential Harmony of Science and Religion**

1. Bahá'u'lláh, *Epistle to the Son of the Wolf*, p. 111.
2. Bahá'u'lláh, *Gleanings*, p. 142.
3. Bahá'u'lláh, *Epistle to the Son of the Wolf*, p. 19.
4. Bahá'u'lláh, *Tablets*, pp. 51–2.
5. Bahá'u'lláh, *Epistle to the Son of the Wolf*, p. 32.

6. Bahá'u'lláh, *Tablets*, p. 26.
7. ibid. p. 72.
8. 'Abdu'l-Bahá, *Promulgation*, p. 316.
9. 'Abdu'l-Bahá, *Paris Talks*, p. 144.
10. ibid. p. 146.
11. 'Abdu'l-Bahá, *Promulgation*, p. 299.

Chapter 7: ***Equality of Women and Men***

1. Bahá'u'lláh, in *Compilation*, vol. 2, p. 357.
2. Bahá'u'lláh, *Tablets*, p. 254.
3. Bahá'u'lláh, in *Compilation*, vol. 2, p. 358.
4. ibid.
5. ibid. pp. 358–9.
6. 'Abdu'l-Bahá, *Promulgation*, p. 174.
7. ibid. p. 182.
8. 'Abdu'l-Bahá, in *Compilation*, vol. 2, p. 379.

Chapter 8: ***Elimination of Prejudices of All Kinds***

1. Bahá'u'lláh, *Epistle to the Son of the Wolf*, p. 13.
2. Bahá'u'lláh, *Gleanings*, p. 289.
3. ibid. p. 217.
4. Bahá'u'lláh, *Epistle to the Son of the Wolf*, p. 14.
5. Bahá'u'lláh, *Gleanings*, p. 217.
6. Bahá'u'lláh, *Epistle to the Son of the Wolf*, pp. 13–14.
7. ibid. p. 24.
8. ibid. p. 50.
9. Bahá'u'lláh, *Tablets*, pp. 127–8.
10. Bahá'u'lláh, *Kitáb-i-Aqdas*, para. 58.
11. Bahá'u'lláh, *Hidden Words*, Arabic no. 26.
12. ibid. Arabic no. 27.
13. ibid. Persian no. 42.
14. ibid. Arabic no. 68.
15. ibid. Persian no. 5.
16. ibid. Persian no. 47.
17. Bahá'u'lláh, *Tablets*, p. 94.

18. 'Abdu'l-Bahá, *Paris Talks*, p. 137.

Chapter 9: ***Universal Compulsory Education***

1. Bahá'u'lláh, *Tablets*, p. 161.
2. ibid. p. 162.
3. ibid. p. 128.
4. Bahá'u'lláh, *Gleanings*, p. 9.
5. ibid. p. 95.
6. ibid. pp. 333–4.
7. Bahá'u'lláh, *Tablets*, p. 130.
8. ibid. p. 90.
9. ibid. p. 52.
10. Bahá'u'lláh, *Gleanings*, pp. 189–90.
11. Bahá'u'lláh, *Tablets*, p. 128.

Chapter 10: ***A Spiritual Solution to the Economic Problem***

1. Bahá'u'lláh, *Gleanings*, p. 285.
2. Bahá'u'lláh, *Kitáb-i-Aqdas*, para. 40.
3. Bahá'u'lláh, *Hidden Words*, Persian no. 82.
4. Bahá'u'lláh, *Tablets*, p. 38.
5. ibid. p. 37.
6. Bahá'u'lláh, *Epistle to the Son of the Wolf*, p. 135.
7. Bahá'u'lláh, *Gleanings*, pp. 81–2.
8. ibid. p. 251.
9. ibid.
10. Bahá'u'lláh, *Epistle to the Son of the Wolf*, pp. 29–30.
11. ibid. p. 24.
12. Bahá'u'lláh, *Tablets*, p. 171.
13. ibid. pp. 34–5.
14. Bahá'u'lláh, *Epistle to the Son of the Wolf*, pp. 138–9.
15. Bahá'u'lláh, *Hidden Words*, Arabic no. 13.
16. ibid. Arabic no. 25.
17. ibid. Persian no. 49.
18. ibid. Persian no. 50.

19. ibid. Persian no. 53.
20. ibid. Persian no. 54.
21. ibid. Persian no. 80.
22. Bahá'u'lláh, *Tablets*, p. 133.
23. ibid.
24. ibid. p. 89.

Chapter 11: ***A Universal Auxiliary Language***

1. Bahá'u'lláh, *Epistle to the Son of the Wolf*, pp. 137–8.
2. Bahá'u'lláh, *Tablets*, p. 127.
3. ibid. pp. 165–6.
4. ibid. p. 166.
5. ibid. p. 22.
6. ibid. p. 89.
7. ibid. p. 68.
8. Bahá'u'lláh, *Kitáb-i-Aqdas*, para. 189.

Chapter 12: ***Universal Peace Upheld by a World Government***

1. Bahá'u'lláh, *Gleanings*, p. 286.
2. ibid. pp. 250–1.
3. ibid. p. 254.
4. ibid.
5. Bahá'u'lláh, *Tablets*, p. 164.
6. ibid.
7. ibid. p. 162.
8. ibid. pp. 164–5.
9. Bahá'u'lláh, *Epistle to the Son of the Wolf*, p. 27.
10. Bahá'u'lláh, *Tablets*, p. 165.
11. ibid. p. 127.
12. ibid. p. 125.
13. ibid. p. 126.
14. ibid.
15. Bahá'u'lláh, *Kitáb-i-Aqdas*, para. 88.
16. ibid. para. 123.

17. ibid. para. 125.
18. Bahá'u'lláh, *Epistle to the Son of the Wolf*, p. 24.
19. ibid. p. 25.
20. ibid. p. 24.
21. ibid. p. 25.
22. ibid.
23. Bahá'u'lláh, *Tablets*, p. 87.
24. Bahá'u'lláh, *Epistle to the Son of the Wolf*, pp. 30–1.
25. Bahá'u'lláh, *Hidden Words*, Arabic no. 9.
26. Bahá'u'lláh, *Tablets*, p. 166–7.
27. 'Abdu'l-Bahá, *Paris Talks*, p. 29.

Chapter 13: **Selflessness and Service**

1. Bahá'u'lláh, *Tablets*, p. 257.
2. ibid. p. 262.
3. Bahá'u'lláh, *Kitáb-i-Aqdas*, para. 35.
4. ibid. para. 38.
5. Bahá'u'lláh, *Tablets*, p. 234.
6. Bahá'u'lláh, in *Compilation*, vol. 1, p. 387.
7. Bahá'u'lláh, *Hidden Words*, Persian no. 40.
8. Bahá'u'lláh, *Tablets*, p. 234.
9. 'Abdu'l-Bahá, *Tablets*, p. 62.
10. ibid. p. 244.
11. 'Abdu'l-Bahá, *Selections*, p. 72.
12. 'Abdu'l-Bahá, *Tablets*, p. 98.
13. 'Abdu'l-Bahá, *Compilation*, vol. 2, p. 415.

Chapter 14: **The Need for Personal Transformation**

1. Bahá'u'lláh, *Hidden Words*, Persian no. 19.
2. ibid. Arabic no. 1.
3. Bahá'u'lláh, *Prayers and Meditations*, p. 248.
4. Bahá'u'lláh, *Hidden Words*, Arabic no. 36.
5. The Báb, *Selections*, p. 56.
6. ibid. p. 94.
7. ibid. p. 162.

8. 'Abdu'l-Bahá, in *Star of the West*, vol. 8, no. 18, pp. 229–30.
9. 'Abdu'l-Bahá, *Tablets*, pp. 305–6.
10. ibid. p. 654.
11. 'Abdu'l-Bahá, *Promulgation*, p. 188.
12. 'Abdu'l-Bahá, *Compilation*, vol. 2, p. 338.
13. The Báb, *Selections*, pp. 214–15.
14. Bahá'u'lláh, in *Compilation*, vol. 1, p. 460.
15. Bahá'u'lláh, *Hidden Words*, Persian no. 42.
16. 'Abdu'l-Bahá, *Selections*, p. 148.
17. 'Abdu'l-Bahá, *Compilation*, vol. 2, pp. 246–7.
18. 'Abdu'l-Bahá, in *Compilation*, vol. 1, p. 55.
19. From a letter of the Universal House of Justice to the National Spiritual Assembly of the Hawaiian Islands, 11 November 1967, in *Lights of Guidance*, p. 353.
20. From a letter of the Universal House of Justice to the National Spiritual Assembly of the United States, 15 April 1965, in *Compilation*, vol. 1, p. 55.
21. Shoghi Effendi, *Advent of Divine Justice*, p. 30.
22. From a letter written on behalf of Shoghi Effendi to an individual believer, 5 September 1938, in *Compilation*, vol. 1, p. 56.
23. From a letter written on behalf of Shoghi Effendi to an individual believer, 21 May 1954, in *Lights of Guidance*, p. 364.

Chapter 15: ***Prayer and Contemplation***

1. Bahá'u'lláh, *Kitáb-i-Aqdas*, para. 18.
2. ibid. para. 76.
3. The Báb, *Selections*, p. 80.
4. ibid. pp. 93–4.
5. ibid. p. 164.
6. Bahá'u'lláh, *Hidden Words*, Arabic no. 16.
7. The Báb, *Selections*, p. 123.
8. ibid. p. 78.

9. Bahá'u'lláh, *Kitáb-i-Aqdas*, 'Questions and Answers', p. 111.
10. Attributed to 'Abdu'l-Bahá, in a talk given to Percy Woodcock in 'Akká in 1909, in *Star of the West*, vol. 8, no. 4, pp. 47–8.
11. Bahá'u'lláh, *Tablets*, p. 68.
12. 'Abdu'l-Bahá, in *Compilation*, vol. 2, p. 236.
13. 'Abdu'l-Bahá, *Paris Talks*, p. 175.
14. The Báb, *Selections*, p. 94.
15. ibid. p. 155.
16. Attributed to 'Abdu'l-Bahá, from the Diary of Ahmad Sohrab, 3 September 1914, in *Star of the West*, vol. 8, no. 4, p. 45.
17. 'Abdu'l-Bahá, *Tablets*, p. 639.
18. 'Abdu'l-Bahá, in *Bahá'í World Faith*, p. 368.
19. Attributed to 'Abdu'l-Bahá, from the Diary of Ahmad Sohrab, 15 March 1914, in *Star of the West*, vol. 8, no. 4, p. 41.
20. Attributed to 'Abdu'l-Bahá, *Star of the West*, vol. 8, no. 4, p. 43.
21. Attributed to 'Abdu'l-Bahá, from the Diary of Ahmad Sohrab, 18 June 1914, in *Star of the West*, vol. 8, no. 4, pp. 41–2.
22. 'Abdu'l-Bahá, in *Compilation*, vol. 2, p. 235.
23. 'Abdu'l-Bahá, in *Star of the West*, vol. 8, no. 4, p. 48.
24. 'Abdu'l-Bahá, *Tablets*, p. 186.
25. 'Abdu'l-Bahá, in *Star of the West*, vol. 7, no. 10, p. 99.
26. 'Abdu'l-Bahá, in *Star of the West*, vol. 8, no. 4, p. 42.

Chapter 16: **Social and Economic Development**

1. Bahá'u'lláh, *Gleanings*, p. 215.
2. ibid. p. 81.
3. Bahá'u'lláh, *Tablets*, pp. 129–30.
4. 'Abdu'l-Bahá, *Promulgation*, p. 238.
5. ibid. p. 49.
6. 'Abdu'l-Bahá, *Secret of Divine Civilization*, p. 103.

7. Shoghi Effendi, *World Order of Bahá'u'lláh*, pp. 203–4.
8. Bahá'u'lláh, in *Compilation*, vol. 2, p. 335.
9. 'Abdu'l-Bahá, in ibid. p. 341.
10. Bahá'u'lláh, *Tablets*, p. 169.
11. 'Abdu'l-Bahá, quoted in Esslemont, *Bahá'u'lláh and the New Era*, p. 98.
12. Bahá'u'lláh, *Hidden Words*, Persian no. 53.
13. Bahá'u'lláh, *Gleanings*, p. 202.
14. Bahá'u'lláh, *Tablets*, p. 26.
15. Bahá'u'lláh, *Gleanings*, p. 316.
16. ibid. p. 328.
17. ibid. pp. 342–3.
18. ibid. p. 272.

Chapter 17: ***Justice and Human Rights***

1. Bahá'u'lláh, *Hidden Words*, Arabic no. 2.
2. Bahá'u'lláh, *Tablets*, p. 27.
3. ibid. pp. 66–7.
4. 'Abdu'l-Bahá, *Foundations of World Unity*, p. 43.
5. 'Abdu'l-Bahá, *Secret of Divine Civilization*, p. 60.
6. Bahá'u'lláh, *Tablets*, p. 37.
7. Bahá'u'lláh, *Gleanings*, pp. 246–7.
8. Bahá'u'lláh, *Tablets*, pp. 69–70.
9. Bahá'u'lláh, *Epistle to the Son of the Wolf*, pp. 28–9.
10. 'Abdu'l-Bahá, *Paris Talks*, p. 154.
11. ibid. p. 155.
12. *'Abdu'l-Bahá in London*, p. 29.
13. 'Abdu'l-Bahá, *Secret of Divine Civilization*, p. 40.
14. 'Abdu'l-Bahá, *Paris Talks*, p. 131.
15. ibid. p. 151.
16. ibid. p. 133.